TALES

from the

GAINESVILLE DAILY HESPERIAN

A CHRONICLE OF A TEXAS FRONTIER TOWN

RON MELUGIN

FOREWORD BY PAT LEDBETTER

THE
History
PRESS

Published by The History Press
Charleston, SC
www.historypress.com

First published 2025

Manufactured in the United States

ISBN 9781467157407

Library of Congress Control Number: 2024944884

Notice: The information in this book is true and complete to the best of our knowledge. It is offered without guarantee on the part of the author or The History Press. The author and The History Press disclaim all liability in connection with the use of this book.

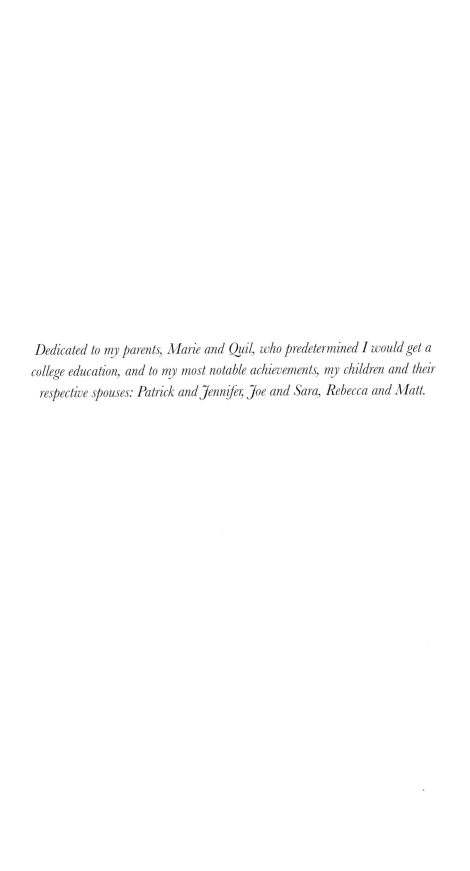

Dedicated to my parents, Marie and Quil, who predetermined I would get a college education, and to my most notable achievements, my children and their respective spouses: Patrick and Jennifer, Joe and Sara, Rebecca and Matt.

Left: Joe Means was editor of the *Gainesville Daily Hesperian* from the 1880s into the 1890s. *From the Gainesville Centennial Program, 1848–1948. Courtesy of the Cooke County Library, Gainesville, Texas.*

Right: J.T. Leonard, a schoolteacher, was hired by Joe Means to work on the editorial staff of the *Hesperian* in 1888. Two years later, he created the *Gainesville Daily Register*, which later surpassed the *Hesperian*. *From the Gainesville Centennial Program, 1848–1948. Courtesy of the Cooke County Library, Gainesville, Texas.*

CONTENTS

FOREWORD

Until a time machine is invented, Ron Melugin's new book may be the best way to experience a slice of life in a nineteenth-century Texas frontier town. Ron is Cooke County's unofficial historian, a college professor and former chair of the local historical commission, and his knowledge of history's big picture makes this deep dive into the everyday life of a community a fascinating trip into the "good ole days." Before the telephone, radio, television and the internet, the local newspaper was how people learned what was happening in their community and the world at large. This compilation of vignettes from the *Gainesville Daily Hesperian* lets us read history as the community itself lived it, while Ron's commentaries weave them into a coherent narrative and a rich cultural picture.

Drawn from the years 1888 to 1897, the excerpts portray an economic boomtown. As two railroads brought in new people and new businesses, the town became an important link between the cattle frontier and the growing cities to the north and east. Hyperbole and exaggeration seep into reporting on the "best" and "most prosperous" businesses, but we also get firsthand accounts of tragic railroad accidents, along with wise advice not to allow "streetcar mules to go to sleep on the crossings." Perhaps the most exciting news reports involve the all-too-frequent train robberies. Even in these early days, the press knew its audience wanted entertainment and excitement, as well as information.

One purpose of a local newspaper was to promote the town and inspire community pride. When a new high school was built, for example, the paper describes it as "the most complete, convenient and elegant school building in North Texas, if not in the entire state." Articles also tout the accomplishments of those who reaped the benefits of boom times and provide details about the mansions being built in what is today Gainesville's "historic district." Social events receive special coverage; the newspaper even printed a detailed list of one bride's wedding gifts, complete with the names of her generous donors.

But the reports also detail a community's struggle with the darker side of boomtowns. They cover the local poor farm and an orphan home's attempts to care for those who were left out of the prosperity. Accounts of suicides appear all too frequently. The numerous saloons in town show up in reports of fights and brawls that end in injury or death, and "soiled doves" (a euphemism for prostitutes) work the streets by night.

This book is a good companion piece to Ron's earlier work, *Heroes, Scoundrels and Angels: Fairview Cemetery of Gainesville, Texas*. In that book, he shares the history of a community by compiling the stories of those buried in a historic cemetery. In this work, he uses local newspaper stories to reflect everyday life as a community grows and transforms. His genius lies in his ability to personalize history and thus give us readers a chance to see the past from different perspectives. He reminds us that history is not just the grand narrative; it is, in fact, the story of all of us, our individual triumphs and tragedies woven together. Nothing does that better than reading contemporary news accounts—"the first draft of history."

Pat Ledbetter, PhD, JD
Professor of History
North Central Texas College
Gainesville, Texas

PREFACE

Unlike my previous projects, this time, through the miracle of the internet, I was able to do almost all my research in the comfort of my home. The Cooke County Library in Gainesville, the county seat, had microfilm of the *Gainesville Daily Hesperian*, but accessing it was somewhat inconvenient. The microfilm reader was sometimes unavailable, and COVID-19 heightened the complications.

This publication would have been impossible without the Portal to Texas History and the Gateway to Oklahoma History maintained by the University of North Texas Libraries. The Hesperian Collection at the Portal to Texas History came from the Abilene (Texas) Library Consortium. After two years and browsing over seven hundred newspapers, I am done.

I would like to specially thank Cathy Farquhar of the Morton Museum of Cooke County for her diligence in finding appropriate photos for this work. Also, thanks to my cousin Jim O'Bryant for his computer expertise.

This book would not have been possible without the diligence and patience of my editor, Ben Gibson.

Chapter 1

THE TWO RAILROADS

A Two-Railroad Town

The city of Gainesville was founded in 1850. The name first suggested for the town was Liberty; however, another town had already adopted that name. Practically all historic references say Gainesville was named in honor of General Edmund Pendleton Gaines, who had died in 1849. Local leader Colonel William Fitzhugh had served under Gaines in the Seminole War in Florida in 1835 and the Missouri Mormon War in 1838.

One event that was significant in Gainesville's development was Gainesville becoming one of a few town stops in Texas on the Butterfield stage's route from St. Louis to San Francisco, beginning in 1858 and ending in 1861 because of the Civil War.

The Denison and Pacific Railway—which later became the Missouri, Kansas and Texas (MK&T) or "Katy Railroad"—reached Gainesville, coming from Denison, Texas, on November 7, 1879. In 1886, Gainesville was no longer the end of the rail line because the Gainesville, Henrietta and Western was built from Gainesville to Henrietta, Texas, where it connected to the Fort Worth and Denver Railroad, giving Gainesville connections with the Texas Panhandle and New Mexico. The MK&T, shortly after that, absorbed those short-lived railroads.

According to the Texas State Historical Association's online *Handbook of Texas*, "By the end of 1885, the Atchison, Topeka and Santa Fe had extended rail service from Kansas to the Pacific coast and was operating nearly 700

The first train—the Denison and Pacific, which later became the Missouri, Kansas and Texas or "Katy" train—arrived in Gainesville, November 7, 1879. *Courtesy of the University of North Texas Libraries, Portal to Texas History, from the Byrd Williams Family Photo Collection.*

miles of track, but it was not a financially strong railroad." The ATSF Railroad bought the Gulf, Colorado and Santa Fe Railroad with the provision that it would lay track from Fort Worth to Purcell, Indian Territory. In fulfilling that provision, it reached Gainesville on January 2, 1887, continuing on to Purcell. About the same time, the railroad connection between Arkansas City, Kansas and Purcell, Indian Territory, was completed.

The intersection of the MK&T and the Santa Fe in a sense, put Gainesville on the map. It would be difficult to overemphasize the impact these two railroads would have on Gainesville. The arrival of a railroad to a town greatly influenced a town's survival and potential growth. If an expanding railroad failed to connect with a town, that might be the town's death knell.

Prior to the railroad reaching Cooke County, many people thought the community of Dexter in northeast Cooke County would be the county's future "metropolis;" however, the MK&T missed Dexter, and it eventually became a ghost town. Wiley Francis Whittington, who operated a dry goods store there, saw the handwriting on the wall, left in 1890 and went to Ardmore, Indian Territory (on the Santa Fe Railroad), where he built the Whittington Hotel, according to the *Daily Ardmoreite* (December 4, 1997).

Both railroads in Gainesville had passenger and freight depots. The Santa Fe had a division headquarters, a roundhouse and machine shop facilities for repairing both locomotives and cars. In 1887, Santa Fe passenger ticket sales amounted to $35,865. The two railroads had a dominant economic impact on the city. Their employees also contributed to the social life of Gainesville. They frequented the saloons and the houses of prostitution in the "Silver City," part of Gainesville. The Santa Fe employees provided one of the better baseball teams in the city.

> The Santa Fe opened its strong box and disbursed about $30,000 among the boys. This makes things a little lively each month. The Santa Fe system now owns or controls 7708 miles of road. At the close of last year it had 894 engines, 639 passenger cars and 23,013 freight cars.
>
> August 25, 1891

> The MK&T will probably commence the erection of that new depot, about which there has been said of late, in the near future, the city council having granted the company the privilege of building a sewer from the depot site to Pecan Creek.
>
> August 9, 1889

> Passengers were as thick as English sparrows in an oats field yesterday morning at the MK&T depot, when the 9:30 train arrived. There was scarcely standing room on the platform, and to get into the passenger depot was simply out of the question; but it will only be a few days till the MK&T will have a new depot at Gainesville, sufficient in its holding capacity to accommodate the traveling public over that road to and from the city.
>
> December 20, 1889

Not to be outdone by the "Katy," shortly after its new depot opened, the Santa Fe built a new depot of brick and stone.

The two railroads came into Gainesville from different directions but converged with parallel tracks on the east end of downtown. The tracks ran north and south and crossed California Street, the main east–west thoroughfare, which ran along the north side of the Cooke County courthouse square. Both railroad depots were in proximity to each other, close to California Street.

Beginning in 1884 and terminating in 1901, Gainesville had a six-car mule-powered streetcar line. It usually operated on a twenty-minute schedule from 7:00 a.m. until 9:00 p.m. on the main streets of Gainesville. When the streetcar company ceased operation, the mules were sold to the British government to fight in the Boer War. *Courtesy of Morton Museum of Cooke County.*

The multiple street crossings were a hazard for pedestrians and vehicular traffic. In 1894, the city had an ordinance that established a speed limit for rail traffic at six miles per hour. Its enforcement was problematic. While fast train traffic was a safety hazard in town, persons crossing the railroad tracks too slowly in buggies, wagons or the Gainesville streetcar created an additional hazard.

From 1884 to 1901, Gainesville had a mule-powered streetcar line that operated on the main streets, usually from seven o'clock in the morning until nine o'clock at night. On one occasion, the streetcar, moving too slowly, was struck by a switch engine, but the one passenger jumped off the streetcar unhurt before the impact. Earlier, the *Hesperian* had issued this warning:

> Street car drivers when driving over the railroad crossing should keep
> a sharp lookout for passing locomotives, and not allow the mules to go
> to sleep on the crossing either.
>
> February 28, 1890

Yesterday afternoon about 3:30 o'clock one of those accidents which the *HESPERIAN* has so often predicted occurred at the Belcher Street crossing on the Santa Fe. Mrs. J.C. Barns and sister Miss Lulu Berry, with her younger brother, were driving across the track when a switch engine ran into their wagon. Mrs. Barns was dangerously hurt, her left leg so badly crushed that it had to be amputated. Miss Berry was badly bruised and the spine injured. The young man was not hurt.

The ladies were carried to the residence of Tom Lovelace where Dr. Conson, the company's physician, assisted by Drs. Gilcreest and Black amputated the limb.

March 18, 1894

Ironically, retired sheriff Pat Ware (see section on "Pat Ware: 'Best Sheriff in Texas'"), who used the railroad frequently in the pursuit of justice, was killed at the California Street crossing near the Katy depot when his Model T stalled on the tracks in 1928.

Both railroads were sued regularly in local court for killing livestock. The following cases on one occasion were heard in N.C. Snider's Justice of the Peace Court. Successful damage claims were brought against the Santa Fe Railroad by L.S. Adams for killing an ox, fifty dollars; by R.W. Adair for killing a colt, fifty dollars; and by E.D. English for killing two cows—he received fifteen dollars for one cow.

Finally, in 1897, the *Hesperian* thanked Alderman W.D. Barrett "for so speedily and amicably adjusting the matter of sounding locomotive whistles in this city."

GAINESVILLE AS TRADE AND RAIL FREIGHT CENTER

Cooke County and the surrounding area was definitely cattle country. It wasn't coincidental that banker J.M. Lindsay influenced the coming of the MK&T to Gainesville. He was also a cattleman. The arrival of the Katy meant area cattlemen didn't have to drive their cattle forty miles to Denison to the railroad.

In addition to the extension of the rail lines, another development that hastened the end of long cattle drives was the production of barbed wire for fencing, especially on the treeless plains of the West.

Joseph Glidden, an Illinois inventor of two-stranded barbed wire, sent Henry B. Sanborn, barbed wire salesman, to Gainesville, where he sold the first of his "Glidden No. 5" wire in Texas to Cleaves and Fletcher Hardware. This proved to be a godsend to local ranchers.

Prominent Cooke County ranchers who provided a large portion of the cattle sent by rail from Gainesville included G.M. "Bud" Bonner, Tom Peery, John Biffle, George Ball, R.F. Cook, John Gilliland, Harvey Hulen, Jules and Jot Gunter and J.M. Lindsay. On June 22, 1895, the *Hesperian* reported that the Katy was loading 112 cattle cars in Gainesville, 48 of them destined for Kansas City.

Cattle trains from further parts of the cattle kingdom also came through Gainesville, some of which used Gainesville as a "rest stop" on their way to their final destination. Typically, a cattle train consisted of twenty cars.

> The freight and ticket agent of the Santa Fe railroad has received notice that 150 carloads of cattle will arrive here from the south within the next two or three days. The cattle are to be unloaded at Gainesville, which is a feeding point for stock in transit, where they will be fed and watered, after which they will be reloaded and shipped to different points of the country.
>
> August 10, 1888

> During the past year there were shipped over the Missouri, Kansas & Texas through Gainesville from west of here to St. Louis and to other northern markets 3,600 cars of cattle, making in the aggregate about 90,000 head of cattle.
>
> December 31, 1889

> Engine #189 made extraordinary quick time coming over the MK&T track from Whitesboro to this place this afternoon. The distance is sixteen miles and it made it in twenty-four minutes and pulled a train of stock cars with it. This is rapid transit for a freight train, but the MK&T track is in such excellent shape that it makes such possible.
>
> October 23, 1891

By virtue of both being served by two railroads and being on the edge of the frontier, a "jumping-off place" to Indian Territory, Gainesville had numerous wholesale grocers, hardware stores and clothing stores that flourished due to their extended markets.

The giant among grocery wholesalers was Tyler and Simpson. In 1889, this establishment occupied two buildings, the dominant one—still standing today—a two-story (with basement) masonry building on the west side of the Santa Fe tracks on the south side of California Street. F.A. Tyler Jr., Confederate veteran, and a youthful John L. Simpson, before creating their partnership, were competing grocers feeding the construction crews of the Santa Fe Railroad coming into Gainesville.

> This firm is doing today a business, hardly surpassed by any grocery house in North Texas, controlling the trade from Gainesville north to the Canadian River on the Santa Fe, and west on the Missouri Pacific and Fort Worth and Denver to Quanah in the panhandle, beside the large wagon trade tributary to this place.
>
> January 29, 1888

> Major A. Van Buren Doak, Tyer and Simpson's commercial evangelist, has just returned from a four-week trip to the Indian Territory.
>
> February 3, 1888

Major advertisers in the *Daily Hesperian* were also clothing stores, which frequently took out large ads on the front page. A number of clothing merchants made trips to New York to acquire the latest fashions for the fall and spring seasons.

Two major Gainesville manufacturers whose products enjoyed wide distribution by rail were the Gainesville Pressed Brick Company, headed by C. Newcome Stevens, and the Apollo Bottle Works. The brick company, according to the *Hesperian*, was "the best brick manufacturing establishment in the state." In 1889, it manufactured a total of three million bricks.

> The Gainesville Pressed Brick Company shipped 100,000 brick to Dallas last week, to be used in a new bank building which is under construction in that city.
>
> November 26, 1889

> Col. C.N. Stevens went to Denison yesterday to close a deal in that city for 3,500,000 bricks, which it is claimed are to be used in the erection of the cotton factory building to be put up this spring. Col. Stevens has large orders for brick from parties in Dallas, Fort Worth, McKinney, Henrietta, St. Jo and other cities in North Texas.
>
> February 11, 1890

The Apollo Bottling Works, according to the *Hesperian,* manufactured the "latest improved carbonated drinks" in Texas. Two of its more popular drinks were crab apple champagne club soda and California cider.

> The works have a capacity of ninety dozen bottles per hour when run to the limit. These fine drinks put up in neat boxes with pretty and tasty labels are no poor advertisement for Gainesville as they are sent all over the country.
>
> June 21, 1893

During the last two decades of the 1800s, because of the prevalence of wheat farmers in the area, Gainesville was the home of two major mills: J.O.A. Whaley's steam-powered flour mill on South Lindsay Street and the Brady Brothers flour mill. Whaley was another native of Tennessee. When the Brady brothers' mill was built in 1888, it could process 250 bushels of wheat a day and had a capacity of 85,000 bushels.

> Under the new tariff rate it will cost 11.4 cents to haul a bushel of wheat from Gainesville to Galveston. One hundred pounds of flour can be taken for 21 cents.
>
> August 18, 1891

The *Hesperian* also noted rail shipments from Gainesville of poultry to Chicago and potatoes destined for Omaha. It was envious of what it called the largest shipment ever of pickles in the United States, from Pittsburg in East Texas to Kansas City.

Gainesville as Passenger Service Hub

If you wanted to come to Texas from Kansas City by rail, you had a choice: you could come by the MK&T (Katy) with Denison as your Texas entry point or come by the Santa Fe with Gainesville as your entry point. In 1890, the two railroads had a passenger train race from Kansas City to a cattlemen's convention in Fort Worth.

> The distance is one hundred miles further via the Santa Fe which had one hour's start in the race. Fast time was made on both roads and the

Santa Fe train arrived in Fort Worth just twenty minutes behind the other, notwithstanding the Santa Fe lost one hour and forty minutes enroute, caused by the engine getting out of repair.

March 15, 1890

The Santa Fe train, on its way back to Kansas City, stopped in Gainesville for breakfast at the Lindsay House, the most prestigious hotel in Gainesville. One of the passengers remarked, "This is the first good meal we have had since we came into this state" (March 18, 1890).

The *Hesperian* frequently made comments concerning rail passengers coming through, although they may not have stopped in Gainesville or stopped very briefly. They included four Fort Sill soldiers court-martialed for desertion on their way to prison at Fort Leavenworth; Negro coal miners from Kansas on their way to the coal mines in Thurber, Palo Pinto County, Texas; and boxing champion John L. Sullivan on his way to Denver in 1889.

In 1891, Texas had a racial segregation law that made it a criminal offense for Blacks to ride with Whites on passenger trains. This occasionally caused a problem since Blacks could intermingle with Whites while in Indian Territory but had to go to a separate car designated for Blacks when they crossed Red River coming into Texas.

N.W. (Norris Wright) Cuney was a politically prominent Black man. He was born a slave near Hempstead, Texas in 1846, son of the enslaved Adeline Stuart and her owner, Philip Minor Cuney. Cuney was freed when he was thirteen and sent to Pittsburg for his education. He became a civic leader in Galveston and became collector of customs there.

N.W. Cuney, the negro collector of Galveston, passed over the Santa Fe with his daughter the other night in the same sleeper with white passengers. Some people did not understand how our separate coach law was violated in his case. But Cuney always knows what he is doing. He was going to Boston and our interstate commission has decided that this is a matter for it to decide and that our separate coach law does not apply to interstate passengers.

September 12, 1891

On numerous occasions, both railroads gave discounted fares to various groups who were traveling together to and from celebrations of their organizations. That included Confederate veterans and members of the Grand Army of the Republic (Union veterans). Both of these had active

Left: Norris Wright Cuney was born a slave in 1846, son of the enslaved Adeline Stuart and her owner, Philip Minor Cuney. He was freed in 1859 and attended a school for Black students in Pittsburgh. He later became a lawyer in Galveston and prominent in the Republican Party. In 1886, he became a national committeeman in the Republican Party, the highest political position held by any Black person in the South. *Courtesy of the Handbook of Texas Online.*

Right: J.M. Lindsay, judge, banker and philanthropist, was instrumental in bringing the Katy railroad to Gainesville. *Courtesy of Morton Museum of Cooke County.*

chapters in Gainesville: the United Confederate Veterans' Joseph E. Johnston Camp and Samuel R. Curtis Post No. 12, one of only a few GAR posts in Texas. The Colored Ex-Federal Soldiers' Union received a similar discounted fare.

In 1894, the Katy, to attract home seekers to all points in Texas, granted half fare to those home seekers visiting Texas from St. Louis; Kansas City; Hannibal, Missouri; and Junction City, Kansas. Half fare also applied to the trip home.

A significant number of Cooke County residents had come here from Tennessee. A major department store in Gainesville was called the "Tennessee Store." W.L. Blanton, in 1897, organized a Tennessee Club to enlist former Tennesseans, primarily to get rail passenger discounts to attend the Tennessee State Centennial in Nashville. J.M. Lindsay, president of the club, was a Confederate veteran, former member of the Texas House of

Representatives, bank president and dominant philanthropist who donated land for churches and schools in the area. Blanton, secretary of the club, was a prominent Gainesville businessman and later, as a member of the Texas House of Representatives, authored the Blanton Pure Food Act of 1907.

The Swinging Gate to and from Bloody Indian Territory

As noted earlier, the Santa Fe completed its rail construction across the "Unassigned Lands" of Oklahoma in 1887. It was obligated to create towns at ten-mile intervals along the railroad line. This facilitated several land rushes and contributed to the dramatic increase in population in the what was known as the Chickasaw Nation. The significant towns along the railroad from Gainesville to Oklahoma City going north included Ardmore, Pauls Valley and Purcell.

Purcell, one hundred miles north of Gainesville, was fortunate enough to be one of the staging sites of the Great Land Rush of April 22, 1889, which opened two million acres for settlement. Many Texans seeking free land concentrated there.

The Organic Act for the Territory of Oklahoma in 1890 defined two territories, Oklahoma Territory and Indian Territory. Indian Territory was reduced in size to cover the area occupied by the "Five Civilized Tribes" and the area of the Quapaw Indian Agency at the border with Kansas and Missouri. The "civilized tribes" consisted of the Seminole, the Cherokee, the Muscogee or Creek, the Choctaw and the Chickasaw. They covered approximately the eastern third of Oklahoma, with the Chickasaw Nation in south central Oklahoma immediately north of Red River above Gainesville.

The office of the *Hesperian* frequently welcomed interstate travelers, who purchased subscriptions to the paper. The Personals section of the paper illustrated the commercial trade of Gainesville with Indian Territory ("I.T.").

> Sweeney Brothers of Purcell, I.T., were in the city Tuesday.
>
> Gillum Loman, of Ardmore, I.T., was in the city Tuesday.
>
> Frank Murray a prominent cattleman of Erin Springs, I.T. is in the city.
>
> C.T. McCaully, tax collector of the Chickasaw Nation, was in the city Tuesday.

Ben Bird, national treasurer of the Chickasaw Nation, is in the city.

D.B. Cargle, a merchant of Washita, I.T., made a purchase from our wholesale merchants Tuesday.

A. Medley, a merchant of Overbrook, I.T. was in the city yesterday purchasing goods for his store at that place.

H. Moss, a merchant of Wichita, I.T. was in the city Tuesday making large purchases from our wholesale dealers.

February 8, 1888

Gainesville was jealous of Paris, one hundred miles east, because it became the location for a federal court for Indian Territory. U.S. marshals frequently came from Indian Territory on the Santa Fe, accompanying prisoners and witnesses on their way to Paris for trial. They transferred to the Katy train in Gainesville to go east to Paris. Gainesville was much closer to a lot of criminal activity in Indian Territory than Paris.

In reference to the "bloody" aspect of Indian Territory, numerous following accounts illustrate the accuracy of that adjective; however, the *Hesperian* occasionally referred to Indian Territory as "B.I.T.": Beautiful Indian Territory. Over the period covered in this book, thirty-seven U.S. deputy marshals died in the line of duty in Indian Territory. One of these, Deputy Marshal Edgar A. Stokley, was shot to death trying to arrest a horse thief near Atoka on December 3, 1887.

Tombstone of Deputy Marshal Edgar A. Stokley in Fairview Cemetery, Gainesville. *Photo by author.*

Deputy U.S. Marshal M.A. Moody, the officer who killed the notorious Bill Towerly, recently near Atoka, I.T., at the time which the outlaw killed Deputy Marshal Ed Stokley was in the city Tuesday evening on his way from Fort Smith, where he had been to take a lot of prisoners. He is headed to White Bead Hill, I.T., where he is to meet with the accustomed party of deputy U.S. marshals, preparatory to swooping down upon more desperadoes of the lawbreakers' paradise. The Indian Territory, through the vigilance of the U.S. marshals, is becoming much more like a hades for those evil doers, than a New Jerusalem.

February 1, 1888

Among the Indian Territory hardened criminal element stopping in Gainesville on their way to federal court was Frank Capel, who killed his lover, Minnie Odell, by bludgeoning her with his pistol and stomping on her prostrate body. A common occurrence was the transportation of Indian Territory lawbreakers who were accused of "introducing" liquor to the territory or stealing horses or livestock.

One potential teenage miscreant was transported from Ardmore to his parents' home in Clarksville, Texas.

Deputy U.S. Marshal S.L. Fry of Ardmore, I.T. passed through the city Wednesday morning on his way to Clarksville, Red River County, having in charge Leon Henson, a youth who recently took Horace Greeley's advice and went west armed with a shotgun and a scalping knife, where he expected to slay thousands of red skins.

The young man took up his quarters near Ardmore but for lack of wild subjects he had been reading about in ten-cent novels, he failed to do bodily harm to anyone. His whereabouts being ascertained by his doting parents, they requested an officer of the rare and red-eyed law of the Chickasaw Nation to harness up the wayward lad and return him to his parental domicile, for further instructions in the art of domestic war-fare.

November 22, 1888

One famous lawman who passed through Gainesville regularly was Heck Thomas, taking prisoners to federal court in Paris.

People came and went to and from Indian Territory on legal business often. The purpose of their trip might be to clarify their status as a member of a particular Indian tribe, to establish their right to a widow's pension, to claim a piece of land in Indian Territory or to be a witness in federal court in Paris, Muskogee or Fort Smith. Of course, not everybody was successful in their endeavors.

> R.H. Plemons, of Pauls Valley, and Miss A.M. Plemons, of Fannin County, Texas, a cousin of his, went before the deputy county clerk to procure a marriage license and were refused on the grounds that the young lady was not of lawful age, whereupon they departed for the Territory where they could get married without a license.
>
> August 30, 1888

James Preston Addington (1842–1915), resident of Gainesville, was another one of those Gainesvilleites who took up ranching in Indian Territory. According to the Oklahoma Historical Society, he participated in the Land Rush of April 22, 1889. The town of Addington, which is on the Chisholm Trail north of Waurika, is named for him. He was its first postmaster in 1896. James Addington is buried in Fairview Cemetery in Gainesville.

> Cal Sugg and Press Addington left here yesterday for Anadarko to pay the Indians their annual amounts for pasture privileges on their reservations.
>
> July 16, 1889

> Mrs. G.W. Adams, who was in the city yesterday in search of her recreant husband, after going before the grand jury and informing them of some of the short comings of her old man, returned to her home in Purcell, leaving behind the avowed declaration that she never wanted to behold her husband, George, again.
>
> November 3, 1889

> Mr. Vince Anglin has returned from Oklahoma, where he went in search of a land claim. He reports that he was very fortunate in his undertaking. He routed a "sooner" and filed claim on 160 acres of splendid land near Oklahoma City, which he thinks he will have no trouble hereafter in holding.
>
> January 31, 1890

Cooke County residents commonly went a short distance into Indian Territory as pleasure-seekers. Thackerville was a popular destination for picnickers, both white and Black. Indian Territory was a hunter's Eden.

From "Jawbone," correspondent from nearby Era:

> Last Friday about twenty wagons and fifty people started for the Indian territory grape hunting. They struck camp near Blue Lake in the land of the red man. D.J. Wilson, who had procured for himself the position of high muck-a-muck of the expedition, struck out to find the coveted fruit of the vine.
>
> He soon found himself befuddled in a dense swamp with darkness surrounding him and no companions save howling beasts and hooting owls. It is said that he tore off his clothes and finally borrowed a dress and sun bonnet from a widow lady living in a small cabin and hired her 7-year-old boy to pilot him back to the camp.
>
> August 9, 1893

RAILROADS: GUILTY OF MAIMING AND KILLING

The *Hesperian* frequently published accounts of railroad accidents or derailments involving both the MK&T and the Santa Fe. The causes of these accidents were sometimes weather-related or due to human error. The minor effects of these might result not in injury or death but in the inconvenience of the "train not running on time." Flooding of the tracks due to rainstorms causing creeks and rivers to overflow their banks was an occasional occurrence. Sometimes saturated ground caused the railroad tracks to spread, resulting in derailment.

> A south-bound freight train on the Santa Fe was partly ditched just south of the city limits, on the grade near Elm creek, about 11:00 o'clock Saturday forenoon. The trouble was due to the spreading of the rails. The track was torn up for a distance of 600 feet, the caboose and car next to it were considerably wrecked. It took some ten hours to repair the track so that trains could pass over.
>
> March 23, 1890

Injuries or deaths, especially of railroad employees but also of railway passengers and sometimes railway trespassers, were common newspaper items. The *Hesperian* followed the dictum "if it bleeds, it leads." It spared no details in describing gore.

> The body of Brakeman Joe M. Knox, who was killed in a train wreck near Justin, was taken to Pierce's undertaking establishment where the mangled remains were placed in a metallic coffin to be shipped to his parents in Parsons, Kansas.
>
> This is said to have been the most horribly mangled human body ever seen in Gainesville. The skull was crushed into a shapeless mass and severed from the trunk. Both legs were also cut off, and one foot cut from the leg. The brains and the severed foot were brought here tied up in a handkerchief.
>
> July 28, 1888

Concerning train accidents, a passenger conductor kept notes of when train accidents occurred over a several-year period. His conclusion was that 75 percent of accidents occurred between three and four o'clock in the morning—this due to workers being close to the end of their shifts and sleepy, tired and careless.

In addition, the railway shops in Gainesville tended to be a hazardous work environment.

> A Mr. Murphy, working in the store house at the Santa Fe shops, had one of his fingers mashed off yesterday by a barrel of oil getting on it.
>
> September 11, 1891

> We learn that Engineer Robbins of the Santa Fe had a painful accident Sunday. While jacking up an engine it came down upon his hand crushing two of his fingers off.
>
> January 30, 1894

TRAIN ROBBERIES

In the late 1800s, passenger trains became prime targets of robbers, replacing the stagecoaches of an earlier time. Robbing a train was potentially more lucrative than robbing a stagecoach, but train robberies required more outlaws and more planning. The prime target of a train was its mail car; robbing passengers was lower priority. Train robbers used various methods, sometimes succeeding, sometimes failing.

J.T. Pirtle (1851–1938), amateur detective, acquired quite a reputation for foiling the efforts of would-be train robbers. He is buried in Greenwood Cemetery in Weatherford, also the final resting place of famous trail drivers Oliver Loving and Bose Ikard.

In February 1888, six outlaws on horseback congregated at the Santa Fe's Clear Creek crossing one mile south of Sanger, where locomotives typically stopped to take on water. Pirtle, armed with his "ever-ready 45-long," happened to come upon them in the darkness and hid within the dense brush where he could observe them. The bandits piled large rocks on the track to force the train to stop so they could board it. Pirtle opened fire on them, causing them to retreat. The detective then rolled the rocks away, preventing a "fearful catastrophe."

On a late November night in 1889, another attempt at robbing a Santa Fe train was foiled by a farmer walking the train tracks north of Overbrook, Indian Territory, on his way to board the southbound train there. He discovered a railway pushcart chained to the tracks two miles north of Overbrook and surmised that it was put there to force the train to stop so it could be robbed. He was successful in walking back north a considerable distance and flagging the train to stop short of the chained cart. Armed railroad employees encountered no resistance in removing the cart. The train continued to Gainesville, being only slightly late.

Almost a month later, Gainesville city marshal A.B. Honeycutt and U.S. deputy marshals Heck Thomas, John Salisbury and Bill Little arrested seven in Ardmore and two in Berwyn, Indian Territory, accused of robbing another Santa Fe train. Two suspected robbers were spotted in Gainesville but eluded officers.

> If City Marshal Honeycutt, John Salisbury and Deputy Little actually arrested the Santa Fe train robbers, it will be a big ostrich feather in their turbans, besides they will receive $1,000 each for the bold highwaymen upon conviction.
>
> November 29, 1889

E.F. Bunch: Gainesville Train Robber

Eugene F. Bunch (1843–1892) was born in Mississippi but spent much of his young adulthood in Louisiana. He was a Confederate veteran. For a time, he was a schoolteacher in Amite, Louisiana. One of his former students, J. Leon Pounds, who had relatives in Gainesville, later became Bunch's accomplice in stagecoach and, later, train robberies. Pounds was the stagecoach driver between San Angelo and Ballinger whom Bunch regularly robbed, as the "lone highwayman," over a year's time. A $1,000 reward poster for Bunch in 1888 described him as six foot, three inches tall, slightly stoop-shouldered and weighing 195 pounds.

Bunch was elected Cooke County clerk in 1876, 1878 and 1880. During that time, he buried an infant in Gainesville's Fairview Cemetery on March 4, 1879.

Not only was Bunch a stagecoach robber and, later, a prolific train robber, but he also committed forgery numerous times, with W.W. Howeth, a leading Gainesville businessman, as his victim.

On November 3, 1888, Bunch and Pounds robbed the Northwestern train not far from New Orleans. They took $28,000 but missed almost $75,000 in railroad payroll. At the time, Bunch, who had the reputation of a womanizer, had a female attachment who claimed to be "Mrs. Ellis"—actually Mrs. Littlehale, wife of a Boston merchant who dealt with the Texas wool and hide market. When she was arrested,

> Her baggage was seized and examined. In her clothes the officers found about $1200 in stolen money, a pair of revolvers and a box of dynamite cartridges.
>
> November 16, 1888

> E.F. BUNCH, ex-county clerk of Cooke County and alleged train robber, whose daring exploits are filling the columns of the daily newspapers throughout the country, was a model man in some respects. It is said by those who were his friends, and there are many such in Gainesville, that he was strictly temperate, never using intoxicants in any form and that he never indulged in profanity, even under the most trying provocation. There is a moral wrapped up in this somewhere, if we only knew where to find it.
>
> November 18, 1888

The Robbing of the Louisville and Nashville Train at Flomaton.

Left: W.W. Howeth, owner of Howeth Abstract Company, who was a forgery victim of E.F. Bunch. *Courtesy of Howeth Abstract Company, Gainesville.*

Right: Eugene F. Bunch: former schoolteacher, former Cooke County clerk, bank robber. *Originally published in the New Orleans* Times-Picayune.

Eugene Bunch, the noted train bandit, who in the past five years has held up many trains in Texas, Louisiana, Mississippi, Alabama and Florida was riddled with bullets and instantly killed yesterday morning near Franklinton, a small town in Washington Parish, Louisiana, by Detective Jackson, the tireless pursuer and destroyer of the Rube Burrows gang, and a posse.

August 24, 1892

Chapter 2

THE CITY OF GAINESVILLE

Boosterism

Gainesville

Has a population of 10,567.

Is the eighth city in the state.

Has a first-class soap factory.

Has a steam printing establishment.

Has three wholesale dry goods stores.

Has an ornamental iron cornice factory.

Has the best fire department in the state.

Is a cosmopolitan city of energetic people.

Marketed 25,000 bales of cotton last season.

Has ten churches, and two commercial schools.

Is the most quiet and law-abiding city in Texas.

Has the county seat, excellent stone court house.

Has street car lines, waterworks and electric lights.

Has two depots, a round-house and railroad shops.

Has three National Banks with large capital stocks.

Has a broom factory, mills and a pressed brick factory.

Has fine stone sidewalks and stone street crossings.

Has gas works, carriage, wagon and ice factories.

Real and personal property, assessed value $2,500,000.

Has one cigar factory and three wholesale hardware stores.

Has four brick public school buildings and twenty-three teachers.

Has saddle and harness shops and three wholesale grocery houses.

February 7, 1888

The first two claims made in this list of "Gainesville brags" are gross inaccuracies. According to the 1890 census, Gainesville had a population of 6,594. Gainesville was not the eighth largest city (population-wise) in Texas but the fifteenth. Dallas was the largest city, with a population of 38,607.

The *Hesperian* liked to point out that Gainesville was not a "boomtown" nor a "tent city."

> Let other cities boom if they like, but Gainesville prefers to be what she is now: a steady-gaited, sure-footed, level headed place that goes forward no faster than she ought and does not lag behind at any time.
>
> February 16, 1890

It chided its citizens to stop waiting for something to happen and to "paddle their own canoe."

A case in point was the benefit of having a cotton seed oil mill in Gainesville. The *Hesperian* praised some Massachusetts towns for their initiative in processing whale oil and some Pennsylvania towns for processing petroleum. Although Gainesville was not close to whales, nor did it have underground oil (not yet discovered), it had an abundance of oil that "grows on bushes." Gainesville bailed tons of cotton and was missing out on a large cotton seed oil market. Cotton seed oil was used as a cooking oil—Crisco originally contained cotton seed oil—and as a remedy for dry skin. Gainesville finally got a cotton seed oil mill.

> At last our people got tired of monkeying with outsiders and came to the sensible conclusion that, instead of someone to come here and build a mill and own it after it was built, they would take hold of it, build it and own it themselves.
>
> Acting upon this idea, a number of our citizens got together yesterday, made up the necessary money, organized a company, and will at once build a fifty-ton oil mill.
>
> January 22, 1892

> The huge brick smokestack at the new oil mill was completed Thursday, and to celebrate the event Ed Woodie, a colored hod-carrier, stood on his head on the top of the structure, a distance of 78½ feet from the earth.
>
> October 7, 1892

In early 1892, the *Hesperian* pointed out to area farmers that they were missing out on a lucrative crop, broom corn. If farmers were "so blue over the price of cotton," they could make between forty and fifty dollars from one acre of broom corn. At that time, there were two small broom corn factories in Gainesville that manufactured approximately forty-five thousand brooms annually.

Two areas of growth that the *Hesperian* promoted was people and money. It consistently advertised the merits of Gainesville to entice newcomers, including foreign immigrants and potential investors in commercial enterprises. In January 1888, officers of the Cooke County Immigration Society met and raised $1,200 to advertise the merits of Cooke County. The *Hesperian* also promoted the efforts of Jay Kimpinsky, a "man of superior business qualifications, and world-wide reputation in the old country as an immigration agent."

In 1890, C.H. Paddock of Gainesville and John Campbell of Belcherville went to New York for six weeks to induce "a number of English capitalists" to invest in Cooke and Montague counties.

Moreover, the *Hesperian* bragged about Gainesville acquiring the reputation of an oratorical and political center.

> Last week she [Gainesville] furnished most of the oratory for her own Confederate reunion and sent Congressman [Joseph Weldon] Bailey and State Senator [C.L.] Potter to help Sherman out on their reunion. From all accounts, Gainesville's reputation did not suffer any at their hands.
>
> August 18, 1891

AGRICULTURE

The dominant economic activity in Cooke County after the Civil War and for several decades thereafter was cattle. Cattle drives came through Cooke County going north, as the county was situated between the Chisholm Trail on the west and the Shawnee Trail on the east. Then the open range closed as local ranchers began to use barbed wire fencing to confine their herds. Farmers tended to grow crops for their own use and sold their excess to a local market. All that changed when the two railroads came to Gainesville.

Wagons of cotton waiting to be sold in downtown Gainesville. *Photo courtesy of Morton Museum of Cooke County.*

One of the two dominant cash crops was cotton. Cotton was king in the eastern and southern portions of Cooke County. Cotton gins and a cotton compress in Gainesville contributed to shipping massive amounts of cotton. Also, a cotton seed mill in Gainesville reflected the importance of that crop. An important annual event every fall was the arrival in town of the first bale of cotton produced in Cooke County. For two consecutive years, 1887 and 1888, Turner Jarrett, "an energetic colored man," produced the first bale of cotton for the season in late August. Around nine o'clock at night, he arrived at the *Hesperian* office to show it off to the crowd gathered there.

> The usual remarks were made, the customary samples pulled and the invariable verdict rendered—good staple, clean packed, full headed, and a premium must be raised for a fancy price.
>
> August 24, 1888

In 1891, Hilliard Fitzpatrick, "an industrious, enterprising negro," produced the first bale. The bale came from the "timbered country near Tioga" on the eastern edge of Cooke County.

Overproduction of cotton, following the law of supply and demand, created a vicious cycle as farmers grew more to compensate for the drop in cotton prices.

> If we could only devise some means to keep from planting too much cotton, all would be on the high road to prosperity.
>
> February 17, 1892

Cotton was not the only overproduced commodity. In 1896, eggs were selling for a nickel a dozen.

Wheat was the other dominant Cooke County crop. The community of Era, southwest of Gainesville, was in the center of the wheat-growing region of the county. The production of the first bushel of wheat for the season was publicly acknowledged but not celebrated like cotton.

> The first new wheat of the season was brought in Monday from near Forestburg [on the western edge of the county]. It was bought by the Lone Star mills at 90 cents. It was good wheat and the yield was about twenty bushels to the acre. There will be an immense surplus to export this year.
>
> June 9, 1891

> The board of trade [the precursor to a chamber of commerce] is having some of the wheat fields photographed. This will be something that Cooke County may well be proud of.
>
> June 12, 1891

Cooke County contributed agricultural products to both the Texas Spring Palace in Fort Worth and the State Fair of Texas in Dallas. The Spring Palace opened on May 29, 1889. An immigration agent for the Fort Worth and Denver Railroad promoted this event to attract visitors and investors to Fort Worth and to Texas. The palace building was almost as large at the national capitol in Washington. Over fifty Texas counties contributed exhibits. Art mosaics were made entirely of natural products. Of the visitors, 28 percent were from out of state, and international visitors came from six countries.

Shortly after the 1890 Spring Palace event, the palace building burned to the ground. The spring event didn't survive. The city of Fort Worth viewed its event as a rival of the Dallas State Fair, which began in 1886.

A collection of green cornstalks, wheat, oats and millet was brought in yesterday morning from the farm of Mr. McAfee, near the south part of the city by Postmaster Pierce, and shipped to Fort Worth to be placed in the Spring Palace.

The cornstalks were 8 feet high, oats about 5 feet, millet about the same in height and the wheat was as tall as Jack's bean stalk, with heads as large as some festive sport after a week's imbibing of Jersey lightning. It was indeed a magnificent exhibit and will literally speak volumes of good report for the agricultural condition of Cooke County.

May 31, 1889

Herman Kaden, pioneer florist of Gainesville. *Courtesy of Dianna Kaden, great-great-granddaughter.*

Herman Kaden, a native of Dresden, Germany, studied the floral sciences in France and Switzerland. He took a circuitous route to Gainesville from Dresden via New York City with a brief stop in St. Louis, where he saw an ad in the *Hesperian* for a gardener for the John Stone ranch west of Gainesville. In 1884, from his earnings from working on the Stone ranch, he spent $258 to buy nine acres of land south of Gainesville to start his floral business: H. Kaden, the Florist. That business, now 140 years old, still operates at the original location, still run by the Kaden family.

Herman Kaden, our Gainesville florist who had been attending the meeting of the State Horticultural Society at Denison this week, returned home yesterday and reports that three premiums were awarded by the society for flowers he had on exhibition. The first for the best collection of named roses, second, for the best collections of geraniums; third, best selection of cut flowers. Mr. Kaden is very proud of his success and it speaks well for our city.

June 29, 1888

When a farmer grew some variety of produce that was abnormally large, he would typically bring it to the *Hesperian* office to show it off and get his name in the paper.

J.M. Parsons of this county took the first premium at the Dallas fair for the largest watermelon. Mr. Parsons lives six miles east of the city [Gainesville].

October 22, 1891

Governing Gainesville

The Gainesville City Council, during the period covered by this book, consistently struggled to rid the city of its "backwater" image and strived to make it a progressive, modern city and at the same time be frugal with its spending pattern. City council meetings were frequently tedious, but occasionally boisterous. On one occasion, one councilman accused the other of spending too much money on a sewer in his ward. That led to a scuffle at the council meeting and the accuser shooting the other twice, not fatally, outside the council meeting.

> The mayor came near violating a city ordinance by sleeping in a public place during the meeting of the council. But he would have been excusable.
>
> June 24, 1891

Under the term "retrenchment and reform," the city council occasionally discussed cost-cutting proposals, sometimes acting on them or choosing to reject them. In a cost-cutting mood, the council in 1888 passed a resolution to reduce the size of the police force. The *Hesperian* criticized the logic of this.

> One of the tangible reasons given in the resolution yesterday passed by the city council for the reduction of the police force, is that there is very little for them to do. The same logic might be applied to the paid firemen. The boys has [*sic*] not had a big fire since Christmas, then why not reduce their force? There is no difference in the reference.
>
> January 18, 1888

The *Hesperian* also noted that the council was serious about cost cutting when it went from meeting twice a month to meeting just once a month, saving the city $500 a year. Later, when the police asked the council for a raise from $50 a month to $60 a month, the *Hesperian* suggested that if the police wrote more citations resulting in more fines, their salaries would be secure.

Among the city government's major concerns were sanitation, livestock regulations, streetlighting, street paving and water bill charges. The proper disposal of Gainesville's human waste—so as not to be a stinking town, and moreover, a health hazard—was troublesome. A city ordinance was very precise in instructing outhouse or privy owners as to their responsibilities in this regard. If the city sanitation officer failed to report any violation, he would be guilty of a misdemeanor and face possible dismissal.

> Article 7—It shall be the duty of every one having or using a privy in this city to place in the rear, for the purpose of receiving the contents of the same, a box or boxes, each from ten to fifteen inches deep and constructed so as to easily slide in and out, under the privy, and shall put a door or cover over the rear of the privy.
>
> Article 8—The owner or occupant of any premises where such boxes are used shall not permit them to leak or run over, and shall every third day or as often as necessary, sprinkle them with lime, ashes or other disinfectants, and shall cause the same to be emptied before becoming filled or offensive.
>
> Article 9—The contents of said boxes shall be removed between the hours of 10 p.m. & 4 a.m. in a closely covered cart or other covered vehicle, to some place designate by the city. All persons are hereby prohibited from depositing or spreading the same in any part of the city.
>
> January 17, 1894

The regulation of livestock in town, particularly of hogs and cattle, was vociferously debated, since many residents wanted to a keep a single pig or milk cow for their personal use. The common problem was how to keep them adequately penned up and unable to roam on the neighbors' property or the city streets. A city ordinance prohibited allowing hogs to roam the streets. In 1888, when the residents near a "hog wallow" in an alley between Pecan and Boggs (Main) Streets didn't promptly clean up their "death dealing nuisance," the *Hesperian* threatened to publish the names of those responsible. Almost two years later, the *Hesperian* again condemned the owners of the illegal "pestiferous porkers" roaming the streets.

The "hog law" was part of a city ordinance that prohibited most kinds of livestock from running free inside the Gainesville city limits, but milk cows were exempted from that prohibition. In trying to repeal that exemption, the Hesperian admitted it had tried to influence a change in the law, but the city council had been immune to good advice on that subject.

> Gentleman of the council, get your backbones stiffened a little and try again. You will not lose any votes by it, for everybody will be over the head fit before the election. Besides, the owners of the cows are "poor widows" and cannot vote.
>
> October 23, 1891

The city council struggled for several years with the issue of providing streetlights for the city. The usual problem that delayed this from happening was the cost involved. The *Hesperian* noted that everyone except "sneak thieves" favored installing streetlights. It favored electric arc lights, not "little pale gas lights."

> We have heard that the city council will consider the light question as soon as the lightning bugs go into winter quarters.
>
> August 30, 1891

In December that year, the city council did pass a resolution to fund the installation of eight all-night electric arc lights for the cost of fifteen dollars each month, to be paid out of the road and bridge fund. However, Mayor J.R. Shortridge vetoed the resolution on the grounds that the money could not come from the road and bridge fund and that the Gainesville Light Company would not approve such a small number of lights. (Mayor Shortridge was a native of Indiana, a Union veteran and a survivor of the infamous Andersonville Confederate prisoner-of-war camp).

In January 1892, the lack of streetlights had still not been addressed.

> Gainesville's want of lights injures her reputation with strangers worse than anything else. Our people tell strangers who come in that the machinery of the electric light works is temporarily disabled.
>
> January 2, 1892

Street paving was another major issue. Most Gainesville streets were unpaved. In 1888, the *Hesperian* published a humorous account of Sheriff

Pat Ware getting thrown from a borrowed horse onto a very muddy Commerce Street, a major north–south thoroughfare that passes on the west side of the courthouse.

> [Sheriff Ware] had enough mud sticking to his wardrobe to start a land boom in the Panhandle.
>
> January 13, 1888

Six years later:

> An effort is being made to have Lindsay Avenue graveled its entire length. It would then be one of the most beautiful thoroughfares in the city. It would also make work for men and teams where the wages are badly needed. Let everyone take an interest in it and it will be done. There is nothing that adds to any part of the city more than gravel streets and good sidewalks.
>
> March 6, 1894

Establishing water rates for businesses and residents was another subject with which the city grappled. In 1891, Alderman H.L. Stuart did a study comparing Gainesville's water rates to those of other "first-class" cities in Texas. Dallas charged a family of five or less twelve dollars per year and one dollar more for each additional person. Gainesville charged eight dollars a year for a residence of one to four rooms, ten dollars for five to six rooms. Both Gainesville and San Antonio charged an extra six dollars a year for a private bathtub.

Gainesville and other "first-class" cities had special water rates for barbershops, saloons and hoses for livery stables. Each barbershop's rate was based on how many chairs it had. In 1891, the Texas Legislature passed a law requiring barbershops to be closed on Sundays. A saloon's water rate was based on whether it was a first-, second- or third-class saloon: forty-eight rate for first class, thirty-six for second class, thirty for third class. Gainesville charged twenty to twenty-five dollars a year for a hose for a livery stable.

The Mayor's Court

Municipal Court

The mayor of Gainesville was judge over the city court and on rare occasions used a jury to determine innocence or guilt. Many city ordinances involved outlawing immoral behavior, which commonly included prostitution (covered in the section "Silver City and Soiled Doves"), fighting in public and mistreatment of family members. These criminal kinds of cases received more attention than civil cases. Fines as punishment ranged from five to one hundred dollars. Those unable to pay the fines were required to work on public projects.

> Mayor Rowland dealt with two sullivanistic disciples [a reference to John L. Sullivan, the first heavyweight champion of gloved boxing] Monday morning who had given a public exhibition of their fisticuff exercises, whereby two heads were made sore and several knuckles badly skinned. Mayor Rowland decided it a draw battle, and charged each $9.20 for his sport. Total gate receipts for the morning $18.40.
>
> January 10, 1888

One unusual case resulted in the banishment of L.E. Secrest to Indian Territory.

> Secrest was charged with mistreating his family and brought before Mayor Kirkpatrick yesterday morning. His wife, with that devotion characteristic of woman, was on hand to plead on his behalf, notwithstanding his brutal treatment of her. She promised faithfully to take her husband to the Indian territory where he could get no whisky if the authorities would release him for this once.
>
> After consultation, the mayor and city attorney agreed that if the defendant would leave he would be permitted to go. This he promised and was released. He was advised by the officers before his departure to let whisky alone and to never again mistreat his wife and little child.
>
> February 15, 1890

Several categories of public drunkenness were illegal in the city: public drunkenness, "drunk and down" and "drunk and troublesome."

There were three cases before his honor yesterday morning, one drunk and troublesome, one drunk and down, and one fighting in a public place. They all pleaded guilty and were given the usual fine of about $10.70 each.

May 31, 1889

Cases involving juvenile delinquency were not unique to Gainesville: for instance, raiding a neighbor's watermelon patch, harassing adults on sidewalks or stealing coal off railroad cars. One misdemeanor offense didn't apply to juveniles exclusively: jumping off a moving railway car.

To aid in preventing juvenile delinquency, the city council in 1894 passed a curfew ordinance that forbade anyone under the age of fifteen from being on the streets after nine o'clock without the company of a parent or a written permit from a parent. On conviction, the punishment was "confinement in the city calaboose not less than one hour nor more than ten hours."

The Fire Department

The *Hesperian* routinely reported fires occurring within the city and annually gave a summation of the number of fires that required action by the fire department and the total of fire damage claims within the city. By 1885, each of the four city wards had its own fire or "hose company." They were very competitive. Each was allowed to determine the style and color of its uniforms.

Two ongoing problems were sounding fire alarms promptly and the response time of the fire department in getting to fires. In early 1892, the *Hesperian* complained about the city's inadequate alarm system. If there was no telephone near a fire, someone had to run to city hall to get a watchman to sound an alarm. If the watchman knew the number of the ward where the fire was happening, he could signal the ward number so the firemen knew which direction to go. Otherwise, the fire department had to search for the location of the fire. The firemen "always get there quickly after they know where to go, and they never fail to do good work after they get there."

On one occasion, the fire department was late responding to a fire because the bell ringer responsible for giving the alarm was absent from his post. The bell ringer was allowed to leave his post for meals, and he was at dinner at the time.

The fire department could respond relatively quickly to fires occurring in the business district. The residential areas were more of a problem. In 1894, the city agreed to have a Gamewell fire alarm system installed, which provided for twelve telephone boxes scattered throughout the city.

In 1892, a tragedy befell the Gainesville Fire Department. A five-year veteran of the department was run over and killed by Hose Carriage No. 1, doubly tragic since it was on a false alarm run. The casualty was Ring, the volunteer fire dog.

> His death was universally regretted, and many eulogies were pronounced upon his life, services and character. Ring was a model fireman, ever ready, prompt and faithful. He was never absent from his post of duty [unlike the bell ringer], and he devoted his life to his work. Peace to his ashes.
>
> March 4, 1892

Horse Problems in Gainesville

Horses were the essential means of transportation on the western frontier in the 1890s, whether one rode horseback or was conveyed by buggy, carriage or wagon. It was a violation of a Gainesville city ordinance to leave your horse untied and to ride "too fast" inside the city. "Too fast" was not defined, and whether you were violating that ordinance was determined by the judgment of the arresting officer.

Strange city noises, especially train whistles, could cause a horse to either buck or run. Runaway buggies were fairly common, whether due to a lady's inability to control the reins of a temperamental horse or to the horse being frightened by something. Pedestrians, especially children, were susceptible to being run over by a horse or a team of horses.

> Yesterday evening Miss Elsa Galatian had an exciting runaway. Her horse dashed down Broadway by Hird, Maddox & Vaeth's and to Weaver Street, then south to California and to Elm and across to the hill on the other side before she could stop him.
>
> Miss Elsa clung to the lines bravely and finally got the horse under control and drove him back to the city. During the excitement Paul Gallia's horse ran away with him, threw him out and shook

him up generally and tore his outfit so badly there is hardly enough left to repair.

July 16, 1893

Yesterday about noon C.H. Paddock and A. Hanson were driving in Mr. Paddock's buggy near the Katy depot. The horse took fright at an engine and started to run. Mr. Paddock jumped out and Mr. Hanson was thrown out. His foot caught in the wheel and was terribly lacerated. The ankle bone protruded through the flesh and his foot was otherwise torn. It is uncertain yet whether his foot will be amputated.

Mr. Paddock was bruised up some, but sustained no serious injury.

January 19, 1894

One horrifying event on a Sunday morning in 1891 resulted in a nine-year-old boy, Lonnie Smith, being dragged to death while herding some horses through downtown on the way to a pasture. When some of the horses bolted, Lonnie's arm became entangled with one horse's rope and he was dragged down the street. His horse narrowly missed Mrs. Jesse Scott, who was close to the entrance of the Broadway Methodist Church (later Whaley Methodist). After W.H. Garmany overtook the runaway in an alley, he freed the boy, who died immediately.

[Lonnie's] clothing was all torn from his body and he was terribly battered and bruised, though no bones were broken. The crowd took him up and carried him first to Ira B. Puckard's home thinking it was his son. Finally it was ascertained that it was Little Lonnie, the 9-year-old son of Mr. & Mrs. H.W. Smith who live on Ritchie Street a few doors north of the fourth ward school building.

September 19, 1891

Lonnie is buried in Fairview Cemetery.

A Kingdom for a Horse

Cooke County was in the heart of horse country. In 1889, W.W. Tobey, a contractor in furnishing horses for the U.S. army, bought thirty-six horses in one visit to Gainesville. For three consecutive years, agents for the government purchased horses in Gainesville for both the cavalry and the artillery. The army also bought mules there.

> For fine horses, and lots of them, Cooke County takes the cake.
>
> December 3, 1889

Local horse breeders liked to prove the superiority of their horses with horse races—outside of town, of course, due to the city ordinance against "riding too fast."

> The race east of town yesterday between a cross-timbers pony and a Fort Worth's horse was won by the latter. A large amount of money was up, and quite a crowd was present to witness the race.
>
> December 15, 1889

Gainesville was also proud of its local cavalry unit, the Bailey Cavalry, named in honor of Congressman Joseph Weldon Bailey, who personally owned a horse racetrack in Gainesville. In August 1893, the Bailey Cavalry, which was only three months old, placed second in a statewide cavalry competition in Austin against much older cavalry units. Their prize was thirty cavalry uniforms and fifty dollars.

Not everybody acquired horses by legal means. Horse theft was one of the most common crimes. Stealing a horse in Indian Territory was a federal offense. There were professional horse thieves who were repeat offenders, and there were "amateur" horse thieves.

> The ubiquitous horse thief: Officer Joe Gaines returned from Waco Saturday morning with August Huffman, the notorious horse thief, who was convicted in the Cooke County district court last April in three cases, two being for horse theft, and sentenced to the penitentiary for twenty years. Huffman was indicted in four more cases of horse theft by the last grand jury of Cooke County and it is for the purpose of standing trial for these felonies that he is brought back to Gainesville.
>
> Soon after being convicted in the district court of this place last May, Huffman was taken to McKinney, where he was tried for horse theft, found guilty and given five years in the penitentiary, from McKinney he was taken to Waxahachie where he was tried also for theft of horses and given five years in the penitentiary.

From Waxahachie he was taken to Waco where he again was arraigned upon the charge of crooked dealing in equine chattels, found guilty and his punishment assessed at hard labor for a half decade in the state prison.

December 29, 1889

Mont Hall of the "notorious McWhorter gang," who was held in the Cooke County jail on several indictments, was allowed to be transferred to the Denton County jail, subject to indictments there. The *Hesperian* justified the transfer on the grounds that Hall was dying of consumption.

One repentant horse thief, whose name was withheld from the *Hesperian*, wrote the sheriff:

> Sir: I deem it my duty to write and inform you that it was I who stole one of those horses that were taken from behind the saloon on the north side of the public square in Gainesville about 5:00 p.m. on the fourth day of November, 1885.
>
> I would like to say that I was converted last fall, and feel it is my duty to inform you of the circumstances, and if you will take the trouble to hunt the owner I will do all in my power to retrieve the past.
>
> I am yours truly,
>
> [name withheld]

February 18, 1888

Another accused horse thief, Lewis Price, was arrested in Bloomfield, Cooke County.

> The horse was secured at the time of the arrest. The sanctimonious thief was attending church when arrested and occupying a conspicuous place in the "Amen Corner." He will be taken to Dallas in a day or so.

July 12, 1888

One very unusual occurrence involved Deputy Sheriff George Womack going to Austin to seek the pardon of Joe Rowland.

> Rowland was convicted in Wise County of horse theft in August 1887 and sentenced to the penitentiary for five years. The youth of the prisoner, he being only 16 years of age at the time of his conviction, and the testimony that went to show that he did not really intend to

49

steal the horse were strong arguments in his behalf and the pardon was granted.

December 20, 1888

And finally, one smart petty thief, J.F. Bells, evidently untied a horse in downtown Gainesville and let him go free after removing his saddle. He sold the saddle for three dollars. Since the saddle was worth less than twenty dollars, he couldn't be sent to the penitentiary for that theft. Stealing the horse would have resulted in a penitentiary sentence.

In the news item below, what was the tragedy?

A terrible wreck occurred this morning two miles north of Temple on the MK&T railway in which four persons were killed, one badly hurt, a fine race horse killed and several cars smashed to splinters.

Two freight trains were running close together when one of them stalled and the other crashed into its rear, causing the disaster.

Mr. L. Cook of Lampasas County was returning from the fair in Dallas and he was seriously hurt in the back and head. His rider, W.R. Greer, was killed outright, as was a negro boy and two white men thought to be tramps. Neither of the three have been identified. The horse was valued at $2,000.

November 6, 1891

MAD STONES

A mad stone was a calcified hairball found in the stomach of a cud-chewing animal. A mad stone was considered very potent if from a deer, even more so a white deer. In the late 1800s, such hairballs were considered to have "magical powers" and were used to cure rabies or other poisonous effects of animal bites.

The mad stone was soaked in warm milk before it was applied to the wound. If the bite was poisonous, the hairball would stick to the wound, draw the poison out and then fall off the bite. If the hairball didn't adhere to the bite, it wasn't

A mad stone, said to have the ability to suck out poison from a wound, commonly a rabid bite. *Courtesy of National Museum of Health and Science.*

poisonous. After a successful application, the mad stone was soaked again in warm milk to remove the poison and make it ready for its next use.

A "code of ethics" associated with mad stones stipulated that the owner of a mad stone could not sell it. If it were sold, it was thought to lose its medicinal power.

There were numerous references in the *Hesperian* to people coming to Gainesville for treatment with a mad stone. W.L. Fletcher was the owner of the first hotel in Gainesville. The Fletcher Hotel was located on the northeast corner of the courthouse square.

> The little twelve-year-old son of L.R. Hayes, living about one mile east of the city was bitten by a mad dog Thursday morning. Mr. Hayes discovered on Friday the dog was mad but did not know that his son had been bitten. After he killed the dog his little boy said to him, "That dog bit me right here," showing his arm near the elbow.
>
> Yesterday morning Mr. Hayes brought his son to the city to have the mad stone applied, but the stone would not adhere to the wound and it is supposed there was no poison in the wound, the boy's sleeves having saved him.
>
> Mr. Hayes had a wound on his hand at the time he killed the dog, and some of the saliva got into it, and when the mad stone was applied to this wound it adhered with considerable tenacity and, it is thought, extracted all the poison.
>
> December 9, 1888

> Mrs. Dr. Stiver, of Pottsboro, came up Sunday to have the mad stone applied. She was bitten Saturday by a calf which she feared was mad. The calf died, and to make sure she came and tested W.L. Fletcher's mad stone. We learned that it adhered several times to the wound. If this is the case, we feel sure that the lady is in no danger, for we have never known that stone to fail when it has a fair chance.
>
> September 15, 1891

> M.J. Dobbins showed us a small mad stone yesterday evening, which he applied to Tom Williams, who was bitten by a spyder [*sic*] Sunday morning.
>
> It stuck for four hours and Mr. Dobbins is confident that the stone extracted all the poison from the wound.

This small stone was sawed out of a large one some time ago by Mr. Dobbins. The large one weighed nearly two pounds, and was cut into more than one dozen small ones. Mr. Dobbins has several of them and feels sure they are very valuable. If they will extract poison in that weight they are certainly worth their weight in gold.

September 19, 1894

PRACTICING MEDICINE

In this period, Gainesville was blessed in having two doctors who acquired national recognition. The earlier of the two was Dr. Jacob Edward Gilcreest (1850–1926). He briefly attended Louisville Medical College but had to quit due to financial hardship and subsequently came to Gainesville. A Cooke County medical examining board awarded him the first certificate to practice medicine in the county, and he later completed his medical degree. His office was above the drugstore on the north side of the courthouse square.

Dr. Gilcreest performed a very difficult operation of tracheotomy on a little son of Mr. Gist at Era the other day. He was assisted by Dr. R.R. Thomasson. The operation was successful and saved the little fellow's life.

October 22, 1891

Gilcreest delivered a professional paper on "la grippe," which was the popular term for influenza, at the June 6–9, 1899 meeting of the American Medical Association in Columbus, Ohio.

Influenza, la grippe or epidemic catarrhal fever may be defined as a specific epidemic and contagious disease, caused by a specific bacillus. This disease spreads widely over wide districts of the country, causing marked febrile symptoms, is often attended by serious complications and causes great and prolonged prostration of strength....It has been more prevalent since 1890 than during any previous decade, having spread nearly all over the country in 1890, in April and May 1891 and in the winter of 1891–92.

Dr. Jacob Edward Gilcreest

California Street on the north side of the courthouse square. Note "Gilcreest" on a building's awning. Dr. Gilcreest's office was conveniently above N.A. Williams's drugstore. *Courtesy of Morton Museum of Cooke County.*

One of the most reckless things the grippe has done to Gainesville was to tackle F.R. Sherwood. However, it floored him and kept him under for several days. And now he looks as much as a hen-pecked Quaker. This is the only time we have seen him worsted by anything.

December 18, 1891

Dr. Arthur Carroll Scott (1865–1940) practiced medicine in Gainesville beginning in 1888, before gaining prominence after leaving Gainesville in 1893. While in Gainesville, he became the "Santa Fe" doctor, dealing with victims of accidents caused by the Santa Fe Railroad. He relocated to become the chief surgeon at the Santa Fe Hospital in Temple, Texas. Shortly thereafter, he hired another surgeon, Dr. Raleigh White. Together they founded Scott and White Hospital there.

Dr. Scott became nationally and internationally known for his advances in cancer surgery.

Dr. Scott, when asked yesterday by a *HESPERIAN* representative about the case of diphtheria on Denison Street, said that his little patient was better. He said it was a case of diphtheria if he ever saw one. When asked about the disease spreading, he said everything possible was being done to prevent its spreading, and the means would probably succeed.

The case was isolated as much as possible, and the most effective disinfectants known to the science were being used. Sporadic cases of this disease have been treated in Gainesville before and it failed to spread. With proper care we suppose there is no danger of an epidemic.

March 8, 1892

In addition, the *Hesperian* bragged about having an ear, eyes and nose specialist.

Gainesville is fortunate in having a specialist with a place fitted up where these cases can be treated and a physician skilled in their treatment. But she has a man in the person of Dr. W.C. Mullins, who is skilled in the treatment of those cases, thus saving our people thousands of dollars that would otherwise be spent abroad in having them treated. Dr. Mullins is having wonderful success and we are glad to know it, for such a man and such an enterprise are badly needed in Gainesville.

July 23, 1893

ETERNAL CHILDREN

In the late nineteenth century, many children did not live to adulthood. Families commonly experienced the death of at least one child. Childhood diseases were frequently fatal, especially in rural areas where a doctor could be inaccessible—and even when a doctor was accessible, his efforts at healing could be ineffective.

Hattie, the six month old babe of Mr. & Mrs. S.L. Ball, died yesterday at the family home in East Gainesville, after a spell of several weeks' sickness, the result of teething.

August 17, 1889

Tincie Gallia (October 3, 1885–December 25, 1895), daughter of Paul and Betty Gallia, was the darling of the people of Gainesville due to her regular performances on the stage. A year after her death, her father and Harvey Hulen built the Gainesville Opera House, which overshadowed previous auditoriums.

The bust at the head of Tincie Gallia's grave in Fairview Cemetery. The bust has been stolen since this picture was made. *Photo by author.*

At the benefit concert Tincie Gallia will be seen in her artistic Spanish dance, which will be a feature of the evening.

May 25, 1895

Yesterday morning at 4 o'clock while the world was awakening to the joyous Christmas festivities, little Tincie Gallia gave up the struggle for life, and yielded back the sweet spirit that had been lent awhile to make earth less sad.

All that medical skills would do, all the agonizing prayers of her fond parents, all the earnest care of devoted friends were of no avail.

Perhaps the angels that came to sing, "peace on earth and good will to man," bore home with them, the tender bud that for a season shed such sweet fragrance around the hearth and social circle, and gave such promise of future perfection.

December 26, 1895

Because of Texas gun culture and because most families possessed guns, children were commonly accidentally shot to death.

Sunday morning on a farm four miles north of the city, James McBath, aged 14, was shot through the heart and instantly killed.

A neighbor boy was in the room with him when he was dressing and there was a pistol in the trunk. The boy thinking it was empty was fooling with it when it went off shooting James through the heart. He fell against the door of the room and broke it open. He died instantly.

August 7, 1894

After another "unloaded gun" fatality, a little girl was misidentified twice in newspaper accounts: first in the *Sherman Daily Register* as "Purnie

Arnold," then in the *Gainesville Hesperian* as "Purdie Arnold." Finally, in the *Hesperian* account of her funeral, she was correctly identified as Hazel Patrick. Hazel lived with her aunt, whose last name was Arnold and who apparently gave this girl the nickname "Purnie." This child was the daughter of Mrs. Arnold's deceased sister, Mrs. John Leslie Patrick, hence the confusion. She is buried in Division 8 of Fairview Cemetery. According to the *Sherman Register,*

> Purdie Arnold [Hazel Patrick], an 8-year-old girl of Gainesville, was accidentally shot at the residence of Mr. [Christopher Columbus] Swindle in East Sherman yesterday, is still alive today. [Swindle was Hazel's grandfather.]
>
> The ball from a.44 calibre pistol, as stated in yesterday's *Sherman Register*, entered just over the left eye and so far as learned, ranged to the right, but has not been located. It was thought yesterday that the pistol was accidentally discharged by some of the children who were supposed to be playing with it, but today after the excitement and confusion are over the facts are at hand.
>
> It seems the children were playing together in one of the rooms of where Calvin Swindle, a sixteen-year-old son of C.C. Swindle, was told to get the pistol out of the children's way. He went into the room, took the pistol off the table on which it was lying and unloaded it.
>
> The boy thought it was a five instead of a six shooter, as it was. He took out five cartridges and thought all the loads were out. After taking all the cartridges out of the pistol and
> laying them on the table, he counted them to be five. He then snapped the pistol back into position and began to show the children how dangerous it was to play with such a thing.
>
> In showing them he snapped the pistol, as he supposed, on an empty chamber. When the pistol snapped the hammer struck the sixth chamber, which had not been unloaded, and the bullet struck the child as above stated. Young Swindle and the family regret the accident more than words can tell.
>
> Today, while it is not thought the child can live, she is conscious and recognizes everyone. The father of the little girl is here.
>
> January 6, 1895

The funeral of Hazel Patrick Sunday afternoon was one of the largest, if not the largest, ever seen in the city. One hundred and forty carriages were in the procession and an immense number of people were at the residence who did not go to the cemetery.

January 8, 1895

ACCIDENTS HAPPEN

Adults, as well as children, were wounded or killed by carelessness or misuse of firearms.

A young man near Loring ranch, named Sherman Rigsby, accidentally shot himself last Friday while clubbing a wounded cat over the head with the butt end of a revolver. The bullet entered the abdomen and probably made a fatal wound.

August 21, 1888

Tom Hayes, a farmer residing near White Bead, I.T., was accidentally shot and killed a few days ago while walking behind a wagon loaded with wood, which was being driven by his little son, and on the wood was a loaded shotgun, the hammer of which came in contact with a stick of wood, causing the gun to fire, and the contents entered the face and neck of Mr. Hayes, who was only a few feet from the muzzle, tearing his head almost from his body and killing him instantly. The deceased was a nephew of Uncle Davis Johnson, of this city.

February 25, 1890

While out riding yesterday afternoon in company with Lee Scruggs an accident befell Arch Hunter that came near proving fatal. As it was he lost an arm. Finding a flock of birds, a shot was fired, the horse took fright and overturned the buggy, throwing the occupants out and discharging one of the guns. Hunter's left arm was so badly injured as to render amputation necessary.

October 7, 1897

Wood-burning stoves and open fireplaces used for cooking and heating the cabin or house were essential but were definitely fire hazards.

Mrs. Deems, residing with her family on Cy Farris' farm, some two miles from Callisburg, Cooke County, was fatally burned Monday evening while getting supper, and died after suffering the most horrible pains, at 12:00 o'clock the same night.

The back part of her skirts came in contact with the heated stove while she was preparing the evening meal, and she was not aware of the fact that her clothes had caught fire till the flames made great headway, almost enveloping her body. She screamed for help, her husband being some two hundred yards away at the time, her entire clothing except her shoes burned off before help reached her. She lingered until 12 o'clock that night when she died in great agony. The unfortunate lady leaves a husband and several small children, one of which is an infant.

October 31, 1889

Baby Falls in the Fire: The ten months' old babe of Mr. and Mrs. Bob Anglin fell in the fire at the family home, some three miles east of the city Wednesday morning and was seriously and, it is feared, fatally burned. It was sitting on the hearth in front of the fire place, with its back to the fire, and during the absence of its mother, who was in an adjoining room attending to some of the household duties, the child fell backwards into the fire, the back of its head coming in contact with the burning coals.

The mother heard the little fellow's screams and ran to it and jerked it from the fire, but not until it had been badly burned about the back of the neck and head. There are hopes that the little cherub will get well, but the chances at last account for such seemed very slim.

February 28, 1890

Barbed-wire fences were very effective when fencing cattle in or fencing cattle out. They were very unforgiving to people who ran into them.

A young man whose name we failed to learn, living near Rosston, ran into a wire fence one night recently and received some severe cuts from the barbs. A physician was called in and patched up the gaps in the young man's anatomy, and he is now getting along all right. The wire fence did not require any patching.

August 21, 1888

Barbed-wire fence in Cooke County. *Photo by author.*

Digging a water well or working in the bottom of a well could be dangerous. What was referred to as "damp" was a poisonous gas that could accumulate in the bottom of a well. The *Hesperian* reported a death due to damp in 1888 and again in 1891.

> C.E. Moore, a young man about 21 years old, lost his life in a well on Wolf Ridge Thursday. He and a young man named Johnson and another person were at work on the well which was about twenty feet deep and had damp in it. Moore and Johnson went down at the same time. Moore, becoming affected by the damp called to be taken out, Johnson remaining in the well. Just as Moore reached the top he heard Johnson groan and saw him fall over.
>
> He called the other man to let him down and he hastened back to Johnson's relief. He tied a rope around Johnson's body and had him drawn out. But he sacrificed his own life to save a friend, for he became overpowered before Johnson's insensible body reached the top, and there was no one to go to his rescue, as the other man could not draw himself out of the well.
>
> Charlie Moore was not unknown in Gainesville, as he formerly resided here. He was a son of Ben S. Moore, who was formerly a

citizen of Gainesville. His remains were interred in the city cemetery Friday.

August 21, 1891

Charles E. Moore is buried in Division 2 of Fairview Cemetery. He died two days after his twenty-first birthday.

Because of numerous creeks in Cooke County, death by accidental drowning was not uncommon, especially when heavy rainfall created swollen creeks that overflowed their banks.

W.W. Lynn, an old farmer, was drowned in Cedar Creek a few days ago while trying to ford that stream on the back of a mule.

June 14, 1891

Yesterday evening about 7 o'clock John L. Simpson, W.T. Peoples, W.H. Stafford and Willie Blanton were seining in Elm Creek almost two miles below the court house when two negroes, Hart Record and Henry Greenhill, better known as "Frog," who were pulling the seine, got into water beyond their depth.

Simpson and Peoples shouted to them to hold on to the seine and they would pull them out. Hart seized the seine but Henry failed to get hold. They pulled Hart out, but Henry was missing. He came up again but was too far for them to reach.

As soon as Simpson could get his wading boots off he sprung in and dived after Henry but could not find him. Peoples, too, plunged in and they hunted for him in every way possible but could not reach him. They dragged the hole with the seine but it passed over him.

Henry was a good fellow and his death is much regretted by all who knew him. Both he and Hart were porters at Tyler and Simpson's wholesale house.

Both were good swimmers, but appeared to be confused when they got into the deep water.

Henry had been working for Mr. Simpson and with Tyler and Simpson for twelve years. Mr. Simpson was much distressed over his loss and risked his life to help him, but could not find him. Henry had a wife and two children.

April 21, 1894

Recruiting Immigrants

When Gainesville was recruiting persons of foreign origin to come there, many came not directly from their country of origin but from the Midwest, where many emigrants had recently arrived from western Europe. Largely farmers, they desired cheap land and a warmer climate.

Capt. C.H. Wood returned Saturday from the North, where he went several days ago in the interest of Cooke County immigration. While absent he visited several important cities and towns in Missouri, Kansas, Illinois, Wisconsin, Michigan and Indiana. He reports the prospects for a big immigration to North Texas from some of the points visited most encouraging.

He thinks that Cooke County will have the largest influx of foreign population during the next eighteen months ever before known in this country. Gainesville and Cooke County have been largely advertised abroad and therefore well-known and favorably spoken of abroad and will be most certain to get their share of the northern immigration which will swoop down upon North Texas in multitudes during the coming fall and winter.

One of the principal features that leads the people of the North to seek homes in the South is the intense cold weather experienced there during the past winter.

July 29, 1888

Gainesville didn't want just any kind of immigrant but people of good character traits.

A party of thirty-one immigrants arrived in the city yesterday from Piedmont in Italy, near the city of Turin.…They are a fine, healthy, honest looking set of people, and will no doubt make good citizens. They will settle on Wolf Ridge in this county and go to farming.

Mr. B.A. Hugon met them and will pilot them out today. Mr. Hugon is a cousin to one of them and it was through him that they came.

The Piedmonteese have long been noted for their bravery, industry and integrity, and we are glad to have them come among us. They are totally unlike the southern Italians, and the Mafia and kindred organizations find no place among them. Texas has room for all such. The children and younger ones will soon become accustomed to our Texas ways, but the old men will doubtless find it hard to break themselves away from the customs and traditions of their fatherland.

December 21, 1892

GERMANS ARE WELCOME

German immigrants passed the "character traits test." They were viewed as honest, hardworking and frugal. After the establishment of two German Catholic communities—Muenster, fourteen miles west of Gainesville, in 1889, and Lindsay, five miles west of Gainesville, in 1891—Stevens, Kennerly and Spragins, a Gainesville hardware store, advertised in the *Hesperian* specifically for a "good German boy" to drive a delivery wagon and work as a handyman.

Three of the Flusche brothers, Emil, Anton and August, had created three German Catholic communities prior to coming to Cooke County: Westphalia, Iowa, in 1874; Olpe, Kansas, in 1879; and Westphalia, Kansas, in 1880. The Flusches favored self-segregating themselves from non-Germans in order to preserve their German culture. They wanted cheap land and winters not as harsh as those of Iowa and Kansas. Colonel Jot Gunter was so eager to sell them land that he chartered a special train to bring him to Gainesville from Dallas.

> Capt. Joseph Ruschenberg and Dr. Carl Flusche of Westphalia, Shelby county, Iowa, and Capt. Emil Flusche of Westphalia, Kansas, representatives of the proposed Cooke county German colony, have been in the city since Wednesday for the purpose of meeting Col. Jot Gunter of Dallas, with whom these gentlemen have been negotiating for 22,000 acres of Cooke county lands. Col. Gunter arrived last night from Dallas and held a conference with these gentlemen at the Lindsay Hotel.
>
> October 4, 1889

After agreeing to a price, Gunter committed to donate $500 toward building their first church, a fourteen-by-twenty-four-feet square frame structure with a total cost of $1,000.

Left to right: August, Emil and Anton Flusche, founders of Muenster and Lindsay. *Courtesy of Morton Museum of Cooke County.*

> Mr. Emil Flusche manager of the Cooke county German colony, has had a town site of 640 acres located and surveyed, four miles west of Myra on the north side of the MK&T, 100 acres of which has already been laid out in town lots. A public square, a park, and a square upon which a church is to be built at once, have been laid out. This town site has been christened—Muenster. [Muenster, Germany, was the capital of the German province of Westphalia.]
>
> October 26, 1889

By 1895, Muenster had seven businesses, two blacksmith shops and two hotels. Two merchants were selling lots of beer. Muenster Catholics were building a new church "to be the finest in Cooke County." The new church would be 130 feet long, 60 feet wide and 30 feet from floor to ceiling, built at a cost of $35,000.

About two years after the founding of Muenster, brothers Anton and August Flusche founded the community of Lindsay at Lindsay Switch, nine miles east of Muenster. Lindsay Switch, owned by J.M. Lindsay, had cattle pens for loading cattle there on the railroad. The German brothers bought 9,300 acres from Lindsay and W.W. Howeth. Lindsay, the Gainesville philanthropist, donated eight acres for a Catholic church, school, and cemetery.

Turnverein is a German term meaning "gymnastics club." It also denotes a place for physical exercise. As an organization, it was established by Friedrich Ludwig Jahn in Berlin in 1811. At the time, it was considered patriotic to promote physical fitness. After the unsuccessful Revolution of 1848 in Germany, German émigrés to the United States established turnvereins here.

Turnvereins in the United States became sort of German cultural and social clubs. They dropped their original German exclusivity and became similar to the YMCA. It was fitting for Gainesville to have this organization because Muenster and Lindsay were nearby.

> The Gainesville Turn Verein will give their closing ball for the season on April 12. This ball, like all the other balls given under the management of this society, will be a grand affair. Everybody is cordially invited. Good music and a jolly and pleasant time will be guaranteed to everyone who wishes to attend.
>
> April 10, 1892

By 1897, Gainesville had grown in its acceptance of the Germans from the west of the county, to the extent of having a big celebration for "German Day," a holiday observed nationwide to mark the anniversary of when the first group of Germans landed on October 6, 1683, at the new town of Philadelphia.

> Today is German Day and sons of the Federland have the town and are welcome. October 6 is really German Day, but as yesterday was a Jewish holiday, and as the Hebrew merchants expect to participate largely in today's celebration, the gentlemen in charge of the affair when the matter was first talked of agreed to celebrate on October 7.

The German Day celebration in Gainesville included speeches in both English and German. Among the units in a parade was a Sons of Hermann fraternal organization unit. Sons of Hermann was founded in New York in the 1840s due to the large influx of German immigrants and the need to combat anti-German discrimination. Texas's first Sons of Hermann fraternity was founded in 1861 in San Antonio due to that area's significant population of settlers of German origin.

Personals: "Everybody Knows Your Business"

This is a sample of the Personals that which appeared in every edition of the paper. It is a record of trivia. Notice how many miles persons went from Gainesville to warrant mentioning in the newspaper. One might wonder if enterprising burglars would read the column to see whose homes were unoccupied and an easy mark for burglary.

Berry Scott is quite sick with fever.

Jack Criss went to Whitewright [a distance of 52 miles] yesterday.

Major A.C. Irvine went to Dallas [a distance of 71 miles] yesterday.

Frank Hendrix went to Ardmore [a distance of 43 miles] yesterday.

Will McMahan went to the territory yesterday evening.

Mrs. Lois A. Inglish returned home yesterday evening.

Perry Froman of Wynnewood [I.T., a distance of 78 miles] was in the city yesterday.

Sol Zacharias has returned from New York, where he went to lay in goods.

Judge Hardy of Montague [a distance of 37 miles] was in the city yesterday on his way to Ardmore.

Mrs. R.V. Bell and children went to Pottsboro [a distance of 34 miles] yesterday to visit relatives.

Miss Lydia Cleaves left yesterday morning for Biloxi, Mississippi, where she will spend a few weeks.

Hon. [Congressman] J.W. [Joseph Weldon] Bailey went to Nocona [a distance of 38 miles] yesterday evening, where he speaks today. He will speak at Montague tomorrow.

Mr. & Mrs. Chambers of Sherman [a distance of 32 miles] who have visited Mr. & Mrs. Wood Stonum, returned home yesterday morning.

Prof. W.B. Romine arrived in the city yesterday evening, prepared for work in the schools. Mrs. Romine will follow in a short time.

Mrs. Pratt will leave this morning for St. Augustine, Florida, where she will take charge of the telephone exchange. She intends to make that her home.

L.B. Curtis, formerly of this city but now of Little Rock, goes to Nocona to take a position in the new national bank there. Mr. Curtis made us a pop call as he went up.

Mrs. Jane P. Moore, of Bolivar county, Mississippi, is visiting her nephew N.P. Pugh, Esq. Mrs. Moore is one of the largest cotton planters of Bolivar county and also is owner of valuable property in this city.

August, 26, 1891

CHARITABLE GAINESVILLE

The *Hesperian* regularly published notices about destitute persons, sometimes travelers stranded in the city.

A horse died in Bass wagon yard last night, the property of a family which came in from the west. This left them with only one horse and they were unable to continue their journey. *THE HESPERIAN* learns that the old gentleman was robbed of all his money before reaching here by a young man who was traveling with him, and being without funds he was considerably distressed.

He has a wife and several little children with him and if his condition was correctly reported the family are in destitute circumstances, and need assistance. He is a stranger among strangers, but there are too many good people here to permit he and his family to suffer.

January 26, 1890

The county and city authorities are requested to investigate the condition of a family of movers quartered at the St. Jo wagon yard, on Commerce Street, said to be in great suffering for lack of food and want of medical attention....The husband and father of the family is dangerously sick with congestion of the bowels, and it was thought last night that he cannot recover.

March 12, 1890

Children in dire circumstances were apt to get attention.

Roy Alcorn, a little dwarf, aged 12 years, came in yesterday on the Katy. He had a letter showing that he was from Missouri and wanted to find Rev. Glasco of Leon, I.T. Enough money was made up for his lodging and meals last night.

January 4, 1894

A waif was found in East Gainesville yesterday evening. The child, a boy, was attempting to cook a potato when found. He gave his name as George Platt and said his parents were dead. He was taken to the orphans home.

June 26, 1897

Pleas for help for the destitute were more prevalent in the winter months.

To the Public:

Cold weather is upon us, and the hungry and shivering poor are at our doors. Our associated charities is a new organization and is not prepared to meet all the demands upon it. Every day there are claims upon us and we are embarrassed because of an insufficiency of funds. They are your poor as well as ours, and their presence forces upon you a responsibility you can but recognize.

This is the time for works not words. Of your abundance can you not contribute something to their relief?

We have secured a room in the YMCA building in which to place donations of old clothing and groceries. Cash donations may be sent to the treasurer, Mrs. E.R. Davis.

January 21, 1892

On occasion, individuals were singled out for their donations to the poor.

Miss Myrtle Praigg drew the splendid New Home sewing machine offered by Stevens, Kennerly & Spragins at the fair.

Miss Myrtle wishes to donate the machine to some poor woman who has none and needs it and will make good use of it.

The machine is now at the book store of her father, T.M. Praigg. Mr. Praigg does not like to select the party to whom it is to be given and requests the ladies of the different churches through their aid societies or other means to furnish the names of any deserving women who they know who have no machine and who would use this one....It will be determined by lot to whom it shall be given.

October 14, 1891

The Orphans Home

An orphans' home was founded in 1894, and not surprisingly, J.M. Lindsay, the county's leading philanthropist, was its main benefactor.

> The noblest work that has been done in Gainesville is the establishment of the orphans' home. Let everyone come out to the Poverty Soshul [*sic*] at the YMCA rooms tonight. It will be enjoyable and will help out the institution.
>
> March 16, 1894

> The management of the Orphan Home will in a few days advertise for bids for the erection of their building. A lot has been secured in Southeast Gainesville at the corner of Tayor and Moss streets. There has been some criticism of the location, but it seems to us that the place is a good one.
>
> The ladies inform us that they advertised for weeks for bids for a lot and did not get a single bid. Then they visited the real estate men and tried to buy, but did not get a single advantageous offer.
>
> Then Judge Lindsay let them have an acre block for $50 and subscribed it himself. This is why that place was selected. The lot could not be purchased for less than four times that amount. Besides this, the location is a good one and will in time be very valuable.
>
> Let everybody help the noble hearted ladies who have taken hold of this enterprise and see to it that they have the funds necessary to erect a home that will be a credit to the city.
>
> November 24, 1894

> Mrs. Ike Stevens did not forget the Orphan Home Thanksgiving day. No one had a larger turkey grace their table than the children of the Home. The most generous Thanksgiving gift we have heard of is the promise given the management of the Orphan Home to fence in their one acre of ground. The liberal donor is Mr. Cal Sugg of Sugden, I.T.
>
> November 30, 1894

Cal and his brother J.D. "Ikard" Sugg were among numerous ranchers who called Gainesville "home" but had huge ranches of leased land in Indian Territory. The community of Sugden on the Chisholm Trail in

Left to right: J.D. "Ikard" Sugg, Thomas Cooke Suggs (father of J.D. and Cal), Eli Calvin Sugg. Ikard and Cal Sugg were Gainesville residents but operated a ranch, leased from Quanah Parker in Indian Territory near Waurika. The town of Sugden (now a ghost town), located on their ranch, was named in their honor. *Courtesy of the University of North Texas Libraries portal Gateway of Oklahoma History, from the Oklahoma Historical Society.*

Left: Quanah Parker, the last Comanche chief. A White man once criticized Quanah for having six wives and suggested he should have just one. Quanah told the man, "You pick which one I should keep." *Courtesy of the author.*

Below: The two Sugg brothers, Ikard and Eli, are on the left, wearing matching white pith helmets; Quanah Parker is in the center, astride a pinto horse. *Courtesy of the Oklahoma Historical Society.*

southern Oklahoma was named for them. Cal is mentioned numerous times concerning his frequent return trips to Gainesville from his ranch in Indian Territory.

In 1885, the Apaches, Kiowas and Comanches agreed to annual leases to White ranchers at six cents an acre. Later, Cal Sugg accompanied Quanah Parker to Washington to clarify the legality of leasing Indian land. In 1892, the commissioner of Indian affairs approved an annual lease of 342,638 acres of Comanche land to Cal and Ikard Sugg at a cost of $20,558. Their ranch, 535 square miles, was in size the equivalent to a little over half the size of Rhode Island. Quanah liked to visit the Sugg ranch in the fall in order to gather pecans.

G.H. Ragsdale:
Resident Ornithologist and Naturalist

G.H. (George Henry) Ragsdale, a native of Tennessee, took up farming in Cooke County in 1867 and later served as county surveyor for many years. He was a self-taught ornithologist and geologist and, as county surveyor, had ample opportunity to observe the outdoors. He was a prodigious collector of birds and eggs and supplemented his income as a taxidermist.

Ragsdale donated many specimens to the Smithsonian and was a regular contributor to the *Hesperian* regarding ornithology, the natural sciences and geology. A Texas Historical Marker adorns his gravesite in Fairview Cemetery, Gainesville.

> Professor Ragsdale has a geological collection which surpasses anything of the kind in Texas. It has taken him many years to collect and technically classify these specimens.
>
> October 6, 1891

> Editor Hesperian:
>
> Mr. Robert T. Hill of Washington city, but formerly of Texas and the Texas Geological Survey, has sent in the June proceedings of the biological society. This is a pamphlet of thirty pages of text and eight full pages of plates devoted to the study of fossils of the Upper Cross Timbers or Trinity Division of the Lower Crustaceons of Texas.

Mr. Hill sends out many valuable plans, all of which are bringing Texas into the notice of naturalists.

In this paper he describes and features nineteen new species and subspecies of [mollusk] invertebrates. In casting about for a name for a new variety of mollusk, ostrea franklini, which he had discovered [in the Glen Rose area], he kindly remembered your humble servant, ostrea franklini ragsdalei.

June 25, 1893

G.H. Ragsdale, Cooke County ornithologist and naturalist. *Courtesy of the author.*

Prof. Ragsdale was in to see us Wednesday with a bird that had a bill as long as the populist platform. It was a curlew, and he was stuffing it.

April 12, 1894

THE FASCINATION OF THE CHICAGO WORLD'S FAIR (1893)

Texas towns and counties competed with one another in raising money for exhibits in the Texas Building at the Columbian Exposition or Chicago's World Fair, for the 400th anniversary of Columbus' discovery of America—although it was one year late. The fair ran from May 1 through October 30, 1893.

Over twenty-seven million would attend the fair, which attracted visitors from all over the world. Nations and states competed to be the most lavish attraction. Recent technological advances were on display.

Since Texas was the biggest state, there was immense pressure to have the best exhibits. The goal was to reach $100,000 in private contributions.

The money collected by the Cooke County world's fair committee will be wisely and safely handled. They do not propose to follow the old plan like the man who gave a dime to the heathen and a dollar to get it to him.

September 15, 1891

Having confidence in the two prominent citizens of Texas now at the helm, Col. H.B. Andrews of San Antonio, as president, and ex-Governor Francis R. Lubbock of Austin, as vice president, it cannot but end in a glorious success for Texas. Then, too, Mr. W.T. Wolf, president of the Provident national bank of Waco, is under bond of $200,000 as treasurer. All remittances are sent to him.

With such foundation to work upon, what is to hinder us from pushing forward the work for Cooke County? Remember that the counties who first succeed in raising the full amount of their assessments are those who will be accorded the choice of location in the Texas building. If this county is to make a creditable display at the world's Columbian exposition it must largely depend on the active and energetic co-operation of the ladies.

It is a compliment to us that we are called upon to share throughout the responsibility and the success of the great world's fair. Our most important task is the raising of a certain sum of money, a thing that

The Texas Building at the World's Columbian Exposition, Chicago, 1893. Residents of Cooke County raised money for exhibits in this building. The buildings of the world's fair were designed to be temporary, and most were white, giving the fairgrounds their nickname: the White City. *Courtesy of the Library of Congress.*

most women have the rare faculty of doing when the need arises. Let it not be said of us, we have lost our causing in that direction.

Mrs. C.N. Stevens, President
Mrs. E.R. Davis, Secretary
November 27, 1891

Look out, Children

We want 100 school children, boys and girls attending school in this city, who have 90 cents collected on each ticket for the Columbian exposition building at Chicago, Illinois, to call at our store, southwest corner public square, Saturday evening, January 23rd from 3 to 4 o'clock, and get 10 cents each to make out the amount of $1.00 for their certificate of stock in full.

Stevens, Kennerly & Spragins
Hardware & Implements
January 15, 1892

The world's fair offered countless opportunities for area businesses to sell something.

The World's Fair Travelers

Will need good trunks and satchels. We have them at low prices. Call and see our line before purchasing.

HIRD, MADDOX & VAETH
June 25, 1893

For the World's Fair

Persons who expect to attend the world's fair can make arrangements for furnished rooms cheap by calling on D. Keeler at Bartlett & Keeler's. The rooms are conveniently located and well furnished.

July 25, 1893

THE WORLD'S FARE in Our Store

Is as Worthy the Attention of Gainesvillians as THE WORLD'S FAIR in Chicago

TEA, COFFEE

SUGAR, COCOA

CANNED GOODS

And innumerable good things.

My object is to get pure goods and satisfy my customers with them.

JAKE SCHWARZ, The Grocer
August 20, 1893

Both the Santa Fe and Katy railroads advertised their special deals for taking people to the world's fair. Many of the Gainesville "elite" took advantage of these special offers, but everybody wasn't excited about the trip.

F.R. Sherwood and wife and their daughter, Cora, left last night to visit the world's fair. Mrs. Sherwood and Cora went to see the fair, but Frank didn't care for that. He just went to take them along.

July 14, 1893

The MK&T railway will inaugurate, commencing June 18, fast passenger service between Texas and Chicago.

"The World's Fair Flyer" will be a vestibuled train, equipped with free reclining chair cars, and luxurious Wagner palace buffet sleepers and will be run solid into the city of Chicago.

Train leaving Gainesville at 10:45 a.m. will connect with "The World's Fair Flyer" at Whitesboro at 11:55 a.m. and which arrives at Chicago at 4:20 p.m. next day, covering the distance from Gainesville to Chicago in twenty-nine hours and thirty-three minutes, making seven hours quicker than any other line.

June 25, 1893

Here is what you have been waiting for—one fare for the round trip to Chicago. Don't let the opportunity to visit the fair pass. Commencing August 1 the Santa Fe will sell tickets to Chicago and return via St. Louis or Kansas City at the nominal rate of one single trip fare plus $2.00.

September 5, 1893

Cooke County contributed a huge exhibit to the fair.

The Biggest Hog in the World

Capt. Hannah will start for Chicago tomorrow with Jule Gunter's famous hog. This hog weighs over 1,400 pounds and is a product of

Cooke County, it having been raised in the county. This will no doubt be the largest hog that the park city ever saw. It will be a credit to Texas and an interesting feature at the fair.

Mr. Gunter has no idea of selling the animal but will bring him back to Texas and keep on the Cooke County farm.

July 18, 1893

NOSTALGIA FOR THE "LOST CAUSE"

Both Confederate veterans and Union veterans had their respective organizations in Gainesville. Of course, the Confederate veterans were larger in numbers than their counterparts and in some of their commemorations invited their former adversaries to participate, which they usually did. The people of Gainesville, in a sense, were very forgiving in that Gainesville elected Henry E. Schopmeyer, commander of the local Grand Army of the Republic post, to several terms on the city council in the 1880s. Schopmeyer Street is a reminder of his influence on city government.

The organization of Confederate veterans was the Joseph E. Johnston Camp of Confederate Veterans. Brigadier General Johnston, native of Virginia, never suffered outright defeat as a Confederate general. He led the Confederate victory at the First Battle of Bull Run. His later strategy in fighting was "planned withdrawal," and he harassed General Sherman in his "march to the sea."

The Confederate veterans had annual reunions locally, statewide and nationally. Ironically, the Joseph E. Johnston Camp was always conspicuous at Fourth of July celebrations.

The organization of Union veterans was the Grand Army of the Republic. Gainesville's Samuel R. Curtis Post No. 14 is named for a Union major general who was in charge of the Union victories at Pea Ridge, Arkansas and Westport, Missouri. As a member of Congress from 1856 to 1861, Curtis promoted the idea of a transcontinental railroad, and he worked for the Union Pacific Railroad after the war.

Schopmeyer gave a moving account in the *Hesperian* of the death and funeral of a GAR member, Silas Taylor, who had recently moved from Kansas to Cooke County. Ill and destitute, he was placed on the second floor of the rural home of Sol Turner, where "Dr. Bell of our city was called to wait upon him, but failed to stay the iron-heeled monster, Death."

A group of GAR members, which consisted of H.E. Schopmeyer, J.R. McFarren, C.C. Sanborn, D.C. Durland, J.M. Pringle and G.L. Carter, traveled three hours over rough roads to pay their respects.

> After trying to comfort the bereaved ones the demands of the bereaved were cancelled by the members of the post, when the deceased was carefully and skillfully let down by ropes from the second story and conveyed two and a half miles to the grave yard and placed in its last resting place.
>
> After the burial, they would now turn in charity to the wants of the living and bereaved, appealing to southern as well as northern soldiers and citizens, and in less than five minutes there was a response of $22 for the benefit of the bereaved widow from those noble warm-hearted citizens. Many tears of sympathy were shed in the closing scenes of the ceremony. The GAR gave a last and final farewell to their departed comrade by shaking hands across the grave, commending him to God, which was very solemn and imposing.
>
> March 19, 1889

When Jefferson Davis, former president of the Confederacy, died on December 6, 1889, Gainesville treated his death like that of a national hero. Many homes were draped in black. An elaborate parade was organized, which ended at the waterworks park, where flowery speeches overflowed.

> The procession was headed by the Gate City band, which was followed by the fire department, with trucks appropriately decorated, and it in turn by several civic societies, the children of the city schools, and citizens on foot and in carriages. At 1 o'clock the procession moved toward the waterworks park, the band playing a solemn funeral march.
>
> At the Lindsay House a Confederate flag with Mr. Davis' portrait in the centre of the field, was suspended across California street, and as the crowd passed under it almost every head was bared in token of the respect to the great original of the picture and possibly fond memories of the cause that ensign once represented.
>
> December 12, 1889

The Glorious Fourth

Look at us. See our confederate reunion today. This makes us prouder than ever. A government that those old confederates led by Lee, Jackson, Johnston, and Longstreet, and others, couldn't down is a good one. No one else need try it. Put those old confeds with the men they could not down and it would make a team that would beat the world.

No wonder we want plenty of elbow room. We need Alaska for a cooling off place, and we will soon have to take in Cuba for a winter resort.

We have more republicans, more democrats, more populists, more anarchists and negroes than any land beneath the sun. What other country can boast of having to call congress together to stop making so much money? What other country can swallow every race, every ism, every sect, and yet preserve our calm and unruffled exterior?

July 4, 1893

About Our Schools

The numbers speak for themselves.

City Assessor B.J. Apperson has finished taking the scholastic census of this town, and on Tuesday rendered his final report of same to Mayor J.T. Rowland.

The total number of children between the ages of 8 and 16 years is 1713. Of this number 1444 are whites and 169 colored. White males 672, and females 772. Colored males 124, females 145....Out of the number of colored children there are but 13 unable to read, while the whites reported are all able to read.

June 8, 1888

There are 86 public schools in the county and in 1890 there were 4,009 children of scholastic age, and 87 teachers employed. Average wages paid to male teachers $42.50 per month; female teachers $38.85. This does not include the city of Gainesville, which has charge of its own public schools.

September 11, 1891

We have ninety public schools in the county outside the city of Gainesville—eighty-six white and four colored. These schools run on average of six months each year.

January 2, 1895

In the fall of 1891, the *Hesperian* noted the problem of overcrowding in the public schools in Gainesville.

> One thing our city school authorities will have to provide against in the near future and that is our crowding the public schools from the country districts.…The completion of the new high school building will perhaps relieve the strain for awhile, but not for long.
>
> The building up of the Synodical female college and the Gainesville college will perhaps furnish ample facilities for all those from the country districts who may wish to come to the city for their education.
>
> October 1, 1891

A "New Temple of Learning," a new high school, was ready for the 1893 fall term. It provided facilities for the eighth through the senior grade. It featured a large auditorium with the "most convenient style of opera chairs," which would seat five hundred.

> We risk nothing in saying it is the most complete, convenient and elegant school building in North Texas, if not in the entire state.
>
> In the basement are four hot air furnaces with pipes that radiate through the entire building. The basement also contains the water closet, storage rooms, etc., nothing being put on the outside of the building.
>
> The second and third floors are devoted to the school work, and contain the recitation rooms, cloak room, auditorium, superintendent's office, library room, etc.
>
> August 20, 1893

Also, that fall it was announced that Gainesville superintendent E.F. Comegys had been appointed to a three-member state board of examiners.

> This will in no manner conflict with his duties as superintendent of our schools. The duties of the board will be to examine applicants

for state certificates and also determine the diplomas of what schools shall be taken without subjecting the applicant to an examination.

September 6, 1893

The *Hesperian*, in addition, reported that St. Mary's School, under the direction of the Sisters of Divine Providence, had enlarged facilities and that tuition was two dollars a month, paid in advance.

Two years later, the *Hesperian* bragged about Gainesville public schools.

> The blue ribbon on the Gainesville public schools exhibit at the Dallas fair is attracting the attention of thousands of sight seers and stands Gainesville as the educational center. It is certainly a grand advertisement.
>
> October 30, 1895

HIGHER EDUCATION?

In the late 1800s, it was relatively easy to create a college, and countless small towns were home to one, many of which were short-lived. There were no criteria for calling yourself "professor." So-called normal colleges and institutes were created primarily to educate teachers.

> The course of study for the Cooke County Normal Institute, to be held at the high school, July 23^d, to August 18, 1888, has been published in pamphlet form and is now being distributed among those who desire to attend the institute.
>
> It is a neat book, well gotten up, and contains a most excellent course of study. Judging from the preparations already made by Professors Howard and Hughes, in behalf of this school, and knowing the superior qualifications and abilities of these gentlemen, as practical instructors, we anticipate the best normal school in the state will be held in Gainesville this summer, and those who are going to teach or contemplate making teachers of themselves at some future time, who can do so, should attend this practical school of wholesome instruction.
>
> July 18, 1888

Confederate captain Thaddeus Constantine Belsher, native of Mississippi, was captured at the Battle of Chancellorsville in 1863. After the war, he established a boys' high school, called the University of Columbus and later Carollton College, both short-lived. He lived in Gainesville for approximately a decade as head of the Gainesville College, also short-lived. He died in 1901 and is buried in Friendship Cemetery, Columbus, Mississippi.

> Capt. T.C. Belsher, one of the most distinguished educators of Mississippi and a college man of twenty-five years' experience, has agreed to locate in our midst for the purpose of establishing a college in our city. The Addington building has been selected and the school will open in September next.
>
> With such a building as the Addington and such an educator as Mr. Belsher and anything like a reasonable patronage Gainesville is sure to have a first-class college....For the present both boys and girls will be admitted and all branches from the primary to the collegiate will be taught by competent teachers.
>
> June 24, 1891

The *Hesperian*, in its common practice in its role as "cheer-leader" promoting Gainesville, was effusive in its praise of the new Gainesville College. Forty students showed up on opening day.

> This is a new institution, but if we are not mistaken it will prove to be one that will bring both an honor and a profit to our city.
>
> Prof. Belsher is an educator of reputation, a man of ability and an untiring worker. He is college bred, thoroughly up with the times with just enough of the old fogy about him to make him require everything to be done in perfect order and thoroughly. When the organization of this institution is completed it will be one of the best appointed schools in the state.
>
> September 8, 1891

Miss Kate Pryor founded a ladies' seminary, which initially operated in the opera house and later moved into the former mansion of cattleman John H. Belcher, an impressive structure on Belcher Street. In 1891, the Presbyterians reorganized it as the Synodical Female College. The college had three divisions: Primary Department, Preparatory Department, and

Collegiate Department. The tuition for a term in the Collegiate Department was twenty-five dollars.

> Some two hundred of our people assembled yesterday to witness the opening exercises of the Synodical college, and they were well paid for coming out.
>
> Rev. W.P. Petty conducted the religious services….C.C. Heming and F.R. Sherwood [were] among the speakers.
>
> September 4, 1891

> The vexed question of rivalry between Gainesville and Sherman in educational matters has been amicably settled. Gainesville gets the Presbyterian female college and Sherman keeps the male college. Sherman's young men will admire Gainesville's young ladies and everything will move on harmoniously.
>
> November 24, 1891

> The Gainesville Female college has given up the literary branch of teaching and Prof. and Mrs. Eckhardt will devote their entire time to musical instruction—voice, piano and string instruments.
>
> January 11, 1895

And in 1893, still another short-lived college was created. The North Texas Business College on the corner of Denton and California Streets used no textbooks but taught "practical bookkeeping from memoranda of actual business, which combines both theory and practice."

> They teach the best system of shorthand in the world—the "New Rapid." They have thirty-five scholars now on the role [*sic*] and new ones are coming in daily.
>
> July 4, 1893

The Circus as an Educational Experience

Towns located on a railroad received a special benefit. That is how traveling circuses came to town. They provided exotic, educational experiences for farm families. The circus season in the South was in the fall, when the cotton crop had been picked and sold and farmers had some cash they could spend on entertainment. Schools typically were let out when the circus came to town.

Barnum & Bailey was the most well-known circus, but it had many rivals.

The thousands and thousands of people who witnessed the parade of Barnum-Bailey's unrivaled show through our principal streets yesterday forenoon, had a treat such as seldom enjoyed in the longest life-time. No description, however graphic, could do justice to the gorgeousness of the display.

The long procession of sumptuous chariots, superbly caparisoned horses, elephants, camels, dromedaries, wild Moors and Bedouins in their native costume on their beautiful Arab steeds, lovely ladies clothed in more than regal splendor gracefully managing the handsome horses which they rode, and hundreds of other rare and wonderful attractions was a revelation of splendid variety and grandeur that dazzled and delighted the senses.

Those who came from a great distance to visit the circus must have felt when the procession had passed that they were paid over and over again for the expense and trouble they had been to. But one had to visit the big tent, which almost covered the eight-acre lot opposite the Lindsay school building, to get anything like an adequate idea of what Barnum and Bailey's show really is, and as there was between 5,000 and 7,000 people at each performance, afternoon and night, this must have been the general conviction.

October 7, 1888

At an early hour yesterday afternoon wagons from the country loaded with men, women, and children commenced to arrive in the city and up to going to press this morning the number was constantly augmented. This great rush of rural visitors is due to the fact that Sells Bros. & Barrett's great show is to be in the city today, and these people have come in time to view the mammoth street parade, and secure comfortable seats, in conspicuous location under the circus tents.

The indications are that an immense throng will attend the great show today. Many of those who have already arrived reside from fifty to seventy-five miles from Gainesville....

This being the first big show to exhibit in our city this year, and also the last one that will be here this season, we bespeak for them an

Poster advertising Adam Forepaugh and Sells Brothers Circus. *Courtesy of the Library of Congress.*

unprecedented patronage. The city public schools dismissed last night till Wednesday morning in order to give the pupils an opportunity to go to the "show," which will be the grandest and most beneficial object less ever presented to the children of Gainesville and from which they can derive more practical knowledge of natural history, Roman history and modern wonders than they could possibly achieve in any other manner, and all for a trifling cost and little time.

October 22, 1889

In conversation with a representative of the great Adam Forepaugh and Sells Brothers enormous combined shows who was in the city yesterday, reference was made to the legislature in placing a heavy tax on the great circus combination visiting the state. He said it would undoubtedly result in such amusement enterprises giving the state a wide berth hereafter.

"It is impossible to change the plans of a great aggregation such as ours whose season is half through, so we will make Texas, though with an estimated loss of many thousands of dollars. But it will be the last chance your people will enjoy of seeing a really great circus while the present law remains on your statute books. I think the law is a mistake.

"The educational value of such an enterprise as ours is incalculable. There the rarest specimens of the animal creation from the remotest quarters of the globe, are to be seen in the flesh while lecturers explain their habits and peculiarities, while in the ring the possibilities of the training of these animals and the marvelous dexterity acquired by the acrobats and gymnasts is a revelation."

September 12, 1897

How Our Upper Class Lives

The *Hesperian* offered glimpses of how the upper class lived by its news about marriages, wedding presents, new homes, or special social events.

> The most costly wedding presents given to Miss Nellie Peery were purchased at the China Hall. Among the most elegant and valuable were purchased by General [William] Hudson and [George McKenzie] "Bud" Bonner, also a number of valuable ones by others.
>
> February 17, 1888

> THE HESPERIAN society reporter has resigned his position in disgust. No parties, no balls, no weddings, no babies even to call forth the richness of his dainty fancy and stimulate his graphic pen—nothing but Lenten rigors and penitential ashes and sack-clothe, things which his gladsome soul abhors, was taking place in the once festive Gainesville, and so he has set out to find other fields more suited to his genius.
>
> March 23, 1890

> The high tea given by Mrs. C. Newcomb Stevens at the elegant home corner Church and Denton streets yesterday evening was one that did credit to her, and, if possible, increased her well-earned reputation as an entertainer.
>
> May 17, 1894

Typically, the *Hesperian* was effusive in reporting about marriages that spotlighted the Gainesville elite.

> The marriage of Miss Lulu Robinson and Charles H. Paddock at the Christian church last night was one of the most beautiful and elegant affairs ever witnessed in Gainesville. The decorations of the church were splendid, surpassing anything of the kind ever seen in the city.
>
> In front of the altar Rev. H.B. Davis met them and performed the ceremony in a neat, graceful and impressive manner.
>
> The bride is one of Gainesville's most popular and accomplished daughters, whose friends are only limited by the number of her acquaintances.

The groom is also a favorite here, and no young couple ever started out with more sincere wishes for their happiness and prosperity. They will leave this morning for San Francisco, and will spend some time in San Jose before returning to Gainesville. They will make their home here. Mr. Paddock having purchased the elegant Wilson residence two miles north of the city.

October 1, 1889

Charles H. Paddock, for several years, was the station agent for the Santa Fe railroad and later managed the Lindsay Hotel. The union of Lulu and Charles produced a son, Charles "Charley" William Paddock. Because Charley was a sickly boy, the family moved to California to improve his health. The move worked. As an adult, he always presented himself as a California native and never publicly acknowledged his Texas roots.

Charley ultimately became the "world's fastest human." He won gold and silver in the 100-meter and 200-meter dashes in the 1920 Olympics in Antwerp, Belgium. He died in 1943 in a military plane crash near Sitka, Alaska.

WHEN DR. ARTHUR CARROLL Scott built an impressive house, it was probably in anticipation of his upcoming marriage to Maud Sherwood.

The new residence of Dr. Scott to be erected soon on Scott and Cottonwood [now North Denton] streets, will be a two-story frame 38x45 ft., with a large tower, brick foundation, and contains eight very large rooms, together with bath room, baggage room, closets, etc. It will, when completed be one of the most elegant and most convenient houses in the city.

June 19, 1889

By the request of a large number of friends of Dr. A.C. Scott and wife, THE HESPERIAN reproduces the list of wedding presents received by this popular couple on the evening of their marriage, to which are also added those which have been received since the first list was published, making a complete list, which indeed is very elaborate and many of the articles enumerated are both rare and costly.

November 3, 1889

In the newspaper article quoted earlier, approximately eighty gifts were mentioned along with their respective donors. Several gifts reflect items typical of the time, including a doulton jar, two card receivers and an autumn leaf pen wiper.

JOHN L. SIMPSON SR. lived for a while in an apartment that was inside his Tyler and Simpson wholesale grocery building.

> The most handsome and luxurious bachelor apartments in the South are those being fitted up for John L. Simpson in the new Tyler and Simpson building.
>
> November 21, 1889

Simpson did not remain a bachelor for long. He married socialite Ida Cleaves in 1892. She was the daughter of Frank L. Cleaves, one of the multitude of California forty-niners who didn't stay in California. He did pay his stagecoach fare from Sacramento to Gainesville in 1858 with gold dust. Around 1875, Cleaves and Henry B. Fletcher created the dominant hardware and farm implement store in Gainesville, Cleaves & Fletcher. It covered the whole block east of the courthouse, bounded by California, Rusk, Bogg (now Main Street) and South Dixon Streets.

Simpson, like Dr. Scott, built a new home for his bride, which was on the corner of California and Clements Streets. The *Hesperian* judged it to be "certainly one of the most beautiful and convenient homes in the state and…finished with splendid taste." The emphasis on "convenient" is a reference to indoor plumbing.

> It is equal in design and finish to anything we have seen in a long time, and with the exception of Hon. W.O. Davis' new residence, which is not yet completed, it is the costliest residence that has been built in Gainesville. It is furnished in a style that is in keeping with the house. In this the excellent taste of Mrs. Simpson is shown.
>
> December 18, 1892

In 1894, the upcoming marriage of Dr. Harry Hamilton Forline, a former Gainesville boy, and May McCallum, a teenage friend of Forline's when they were neighbors in Los Angeles, probably received much coverage in the papers in Los Angeles and Chicago because of the couple's social status and the serendipitous twists that their romance took.

Harry's father, H. Hamilton Forline Sr., was a practicing physician in Gainesville (listed in the Gainesville directory of 1888) who later moved to California. As shown by the Charley Paddock story, when the small-town origin of someone who becomes a celebrity distant from their place of origin, their place of origin "clings to their coattails."

The *Hesperian* repeated the complicated story of Harry and May's romance, which was initially told in the *Chicago News*. The following is an abridgement of the newspaper article.

> The secret of a very pretty romance, in which a prominent south side physician and the daughter of a judge of the supreme court of California figure as the principal actors, has just come to light through the announcement of an early wedding in September.
>
> Owing to the high social position of the couple and the strikingly romantic features of the engagement has given the city of the south side and Hyde Park something new to talk about through the dull hours of the vacation period, and the opportunity is not allowed to pass without taking advantage of.
>
> The contracting parties are Miss May McCallum, daughter of Judge J.G. McCallum of Los Angeles, California and Dr H. Hamilton Forline, Jr. of Hyde Park, Illinois. It was all through a visit Miss McCallum made to the world's fair last year and the appearance of the picture of the young physician in the Daily News as the valedictorian of his class at the graduation exercises of the Chicago Medical college that the young couple met after a separation of years.

There was another separation while Dr. Forline practiced medicine in numerous hospitals in Europe, but the lovers didn't lose touch.

> Miss McCallum's father is an ex-member of the state senate as well as a judge of the state supreme court [of California], and is reputed to be immensely wealthy. Being prominent in society, the announcement of the engagement is probably creating quite a stir in Los Angeles as well as Chicago.
>
> *Chicago News*, August 5, 1894

Francis Marion Dougherty (1826–1895) was born in Alabama and moved to Gainesville via McKinney, Texas, shortly before the Civil War. He served three terms in the Texas House of Representatives, first in McKinney before the war and then when he was elected and reelected in 1878 and 1880. As president of the First National Bank, he was part of the Gainesville elite. Dougherty was president of the Gainesville Board of Trade, a precursor of the chamber of commerce, and was instrumental in the founding of the county fair in Gainesville in 1891.

> The funeral of Capt. F.M. Dougherty was largely attended yesterday afternoon. The services were very impressive. One hundred and sixteen vehicles were in the procession. As a tribute of respect almost every place of business in the city closed during the funeral. The following citizens served as pallbearers: C.C. Potter, C.C. Hemming, J.H. Garnett, E.P. Bomar, J.W. Phillips, W.O. Davis, L.B. Edwards, Ikard Sugg, E.F. Scott, T.D. Lacy, F.J. Hall, Phillip Lewis, C.N. Stevens, J.R. Stevens, Billy Newsome, J.M. Lindsay, and W.B. Worsham.
>
> December 29, 1895

FRATERNAL ORDERS

The Freemasons or Masons are the world's largest and oldest fraternal order. George Washington and Sam Houston were Masons. Not surprising, the Masons were the dominant fraternal order in Cooke County. Masonic Lodges on the frontier commonly served as schoolhouses.

> W.C. Hand will go to Rosston to build the new Masonic hall and school house which the good people of that place are erecting.
>
> September 2, 1891

> We regret to hear of the destruction of the Dexter school house and Mason hall by fire. It was burned Tuesday morning. The Masonic brethren had their part insured for $700. This is a sad blow, but the people of Dexter are thriving and energetic and will soon rebuild it. They will no doubt build a still better one.
>
> August 29, 1894

The colored grand lodge of Masons was called to order yesterday morning by Grand Master J.W. McKinney. McKinney was reelected grand master, R.D. Jones deputy grand master and William Crawford grand warden all the unanimous vote of the lodge.

June 18, 1897

Another prominent lodge hall in Gainesville was that of the Knights of Pythias. The Knights of Pythias organization was based on a Greek story about a man who volunteered to take the place of his best friend who was condemned to death, offering himself so his friend would not leave a widow behind. President Lincoln promoted the organization as a way of reuniting the North and the South after the Civil War.

Knights of Pythias, Attention
You are hereby ordered to meet at Castle Hall, Friday, June 23 at 3 p.m., in full dress uniform for the purpose of attending the funeral of our deceased Sir Knight Andrew A. Carrington.
By order of E.F. Comegys, Sir Knight Lieutenant Commanding
[Carrington's] funeral will take place at Denton Street Methodist at 4:00 p.m. Conductor Carrington was a favorite among railroad people....He died at the home of C.C. Walker on Cottonwood Street.

June 23, 1893

Joseph Cullen Root founded Woodmen of the World on June 2, 1890, in Omaha, Nebraska. It was created to provide affordable life insurance, burial benefits and a distinctive grave marker for the common man. Its name is based on the idea that a woodsman's primary responsibility is to provide shelter for his family. By 1898, the organization had over eighty-eight thousand members nationwide.

There are many distinctive Woodman of the World and Woodman Circle (for the ladies) tombstones in the form of tree trunks in Fairview Cemetery in Gainesville.

Dr. C.H. Hobbs, deputy head consul Woodmen of the World, is in the city organizing a Grove of the Ladies Auxillary of that order. He has just organized a Grove at Fort Worth from which points he hails.

June 14, 1895

Last night was "children's night" with the Woodmen of the World. A splendid little folks program had been arranged and was carried out to the letter. The magnificent hall was crowded with members of the order and their wives.

A unique feature of the occasion was an old fashioned brick fire place erected in one corner of the room and in it were placed little "bricks" filled with candy for the children. Fruit was also distributed. The several recitations and songs were splendidly rendered.

The Woodmen of the World is perhaps the foremost beneficiary order in the city and certainly so in regard to numbers and sociability. It is growing fast.

November 28, 1895

The Improved Order of Red Men was a fraternal order created in 1834 by descendants of the Sons of Liberty, the famous protestors against the Stamp Act early in the American Revolution. "It was focused on temperance, patriotism and American History."

According to its membership requirements in 1886, ironically, "No person shall be entitled to adoption into the Order except a free white male of good moral character and standing, of the full age of twenty-one great suns, who believes in the existence of a Great Spirit, the Creator and Preserver of the Universe, and is possessed of some known reputable means of support."

In the 1880s, it provided temporary disability benefits and a death benefit for its members.

A local unit of the order was called a tribe. A meeting place was called a wigwam. The Improved Order maintains a museum in Waco, Texas.

Attention Red Men

On the full moon, about August 25, there will be a grand reunion of the Cherokee Indians of Cooke County. The gathering of the tribe will be where the waters of Elm glide through the shady trees of the Lindsay Park.

By Order of the Big Sachem

August 20, 1893

The Opening of Kanetso Park a Success

Yesterday was a great day for the Red Men and their picnic satisfied everybody. At an early hour the city was crowded. Every incoming train brought visitors and when the hour of the procession rolled around it was almost impossible to get through the crowd on California street.

Arriving at the grounds the people were made welcome by [Mayor] J.Z. Keel in a happy speech. Immediately after the ball game the Hemming Guards and Red Men engaged in a sham battle. The military tactics were mystifying to the majority of the people, but it appeared to satisfy the onlookers.

At night the dance platform was well patronized and dancing was kept up until Sunday, July 4. It was a great day and the largest crowd ever seen in Gainesville attended the opening of Kanetso park under the auspices of the Red Men.

July 4, 1897

Recreation and Amusements

As a public service, the *Hesperian* would alert the public when residents of local fame were performing and the newspaper thought their performance warranted a large audience. Such was the case of Dixie Crooks Potter, the daughter of Thomas J. Crooks of Denison, a former member of the Texas legislature and wife of future Texas senator C.L. Potter. For a number of years, she was soloist and choir director of First Methodist Church in Gainesville. When she sang, she was frequently asked to sing "Dixie," which she usually did.

Mrs. Dixie Crooks Potter, the gifted and artistic "Texas nightingale," consented to sing a solo at the services on Sunday evening. The fame of this accomplished cantatrice is wider than the state of Texas, and to say that she will sing is to insure a treat to all who will be present.

June 23, 1889

Occasionally, the *Hesperian* would announce public performances of Black artists it thought were worthy of performing before White audiences—of course, with racially segregated seating.

Sidney Woodward, the colored tenor who has given several concerts in the city at the colored Baptist church, assisted by other talent, will give a concert Friday night at the YMCA's rooms, by special request of a number of white people who have heard him sing and have a very high opinion of his voice and desire him to be generally heard.

November 14, 1888

A new form of recreation became available to the people of Gainesville in December 1888.

The Gate City Cornet band and orchestra under the leadership of Jas. L. Goben, have put in fine order the spacious hall over the Baum building, southeast corner of the square, in which they will open a skating rink, Monday night, December 10.

They have 100 pairs of new skates (Hendley make) and propose to conduct the rink in a manner that meets with approbation of good people. The band and orchestra will furnish music each evening.

A special invitation is extended to the ladies and perfect order will be adhered to. Admission 15 cents, use of skates for the evening 19 cents extra. Ladies free and gentlemen accompanying ladies free.

December 9, 1888

In 1891, a fair committee purchased forty-two acres on the east side of town south of the city cemetery from W.W. Howeth. That paved the way for a series of county fairs and livestock shows. Over one hundred stalls were built for the first fair. The *Hesperian* bragged that was more than what the Bonham fair had and the Bonham fair was a success.

Friday, October 9 is school day at the fair and every school child in Cooke County will be admitted on that day for fifteen cents.

October 1, 1891

School Day was the "crowning day" of that fair. One of the large attractions was Governor Jim Hogg (pun intended: he was six foot two and weighed 285 pounds).

At 9:00 the governor, lieutenant governor [George C. Pendleton], superintendent of the deaf and dumb asylum, and Col. W.L. Malone of the Fort Worth Gazette, accompanied by Fair President R.S. Rollins, Mayor John T. Walker and Senator C.L. Potter of Gainesville….

As the governor's carriage passed a cheer burst simultaneously from a thousand little throats and made music sweeter by far than the huzzas of the grown men.

October 10, 1891

And at the fair of 1892:

At 10:30 o'clock the baby show took place, and while that was going on in the grandstand the great cavalcade of all premium stock was being conducted in front of the grandstand, and a finer display of blooded stock was never before seen at a county fair.

But the eyes of everyone centered on the baby show. There were twelve of the little sweets competing....After close scrutiny and all the little ones had been kissed several times by the judges, the 8-months-old son of Mr. and Mrs. Bud Bonner was awarded the first prize of $10, and the little 8-months-old son of Mr. & Mrs. William Hatfield was given second money, $5.

September 10, 1892

About a decade after the skating rink opened, a new form of recreation opened, which again required special rules to protect the decency of the ladies.

The natatorium will be open for business Thursday night, April 8, with plenty of hot water, nice tubs, clean towels, etc. Our accommodations are much better than last season. We now have in our tub department hot and cold showers, steam vapors, heaters, etc.; also a private department for ladies.

Buy tickets and save money. We will sell five tickets for $1.00 to be used in either tubs or pool. We give one hour in the pool or one-half hour in tubs for the same. The pool will be used Tuesday and Friday evening for ladies only. Thursday night for ladies and gents— no gentleman admitted without a lady.

April 8, 1897

Balloon ascensions were popular outdoor attractions.

The balloon ascension Saturday evening put the whole city in a good humor. The low price of cotton and the bad weather had been giving everybody the blues. But looking up at Professor Rowe and his balloon brightened them up. Try it again Monday evening.

January 24, 1892

A good crowd attended the celebration at Moffit's [*sic*] park yesterday. The attendance was made up of country people and all enjoyed the occasion. Late in the evening the aeronauts attempted a balloon ascension, but through improper inflation it was a failure.

July 6, 1897

Ned Moffett (1842–1924), a biracial former slave, farmed ninety acres of land on Elm Creek on the west side of town. He allowed picnics on his land adjacent to the creek. After his death, his heirs sold five acres of his land to the City of Gainesville to provide a racially segregated park for the Black community.

Simple indoor parties, usually organized by the ladies, offered a nice escape from a monotonous lifestyle.

There was another candy-pulling at the Lindsay house last night, and fun and frolic were the order of the evening. The boarders know how to make the most of life, and these candy-pullings are indeed jolly occasions.

February 20, 1892

Cobweb parties—a way to show off a house and its furnishings—were popular in the late 1800s. They sometimes required several days of preparation, usually starting with a chandelier, from which ribbons were draped and interlaced, running in all directions all over the house and wrapped around objects and furniture. Each guest was assigned a particular ribbon to untangle from the other ribbons it crossed. Thus, guests confronted each other all over the house.

Mr. and Mrs. Charles Walker entertained a number of friends Thursday evening in a most pleasant manner at their residence on North Cottonwood Street (now Denton Street), the principal attraction being the unwinding of the cobwebs. Aside from this novel attraction there were music and dancing and a splendid supper, all the features, models of completeness in their arrangements.

It is sufficient to say the reputation of Mrs. Walker as a pleasing hostess was well sustained on this occasion, and the assistance rendered by Miss Mildred Miller was most valuable and notably felt among the guests.

July 16, 1892

The Athenaeum Literary Society was established by University of Texas law students on October 5, 1883 to promote debate and public speaking. Its co-founder was Yancey Lewis (1861–1915). In all likelihood he was probably instrumental in creating the Athenaeum Society in Gainesville while practicing law here. The Gainesville club was established at a meeting in the YMCA on September 27, 1894. Later, Lewis became the dean of the University of Texas Law School and president of the Texas Bar Association, according to the *Handbook of Texas Online.*

Yancey Lewis, founder of the Athenaeum Society. *Courtesy of the Oklahoma Historical Society.*

The meeting of the Athenaeum Literary Society in the parlors of the YMCA last night was well attended by an interested audience. The superior merit of every feature is a high testimonial of the ability of its members.

In the debate the question was: "Resolved that the United States have reached their highest prosperity." The verdict was for the negative.

October 24, 1894

According to Wikipedia, the card game Whist gets its name from a seventeenth-century term meaning, "quiet, silent, attentive." A text on how to play this game was published in 1862. The game is very similar to contract bridge, which evolved from this game during the 1890s.

The Whist club was entertained Thursday evening by Mrs. Joe Means at her home on Broadway. It was one of the most pleasant meetings the club has yet had. [Mrs. Means was the widow of a former editor of the *Daily Hesperian.*]

December 1, 1894

The century tea to be given Tuesday, April 13th, at the residence of Mrs. P.H. Lanius promises to be a very pleasant affair. There will be two dining rooms, representing 1797 and 1897. Eight of Gainesville's most charming young ladies will act as waiters.

Mrs. Lanius and her assistants will receive from 3 to 11 p.m. A literary and musical program has been arranged for the evening. An admission fee of 25 cents entitles to all privileges.

April 11, 1897

Gainesville has a strong baseball tradition. It was the most popular spectator sport in the late 1800s.

Gainesville Wipes Up the Earth with Dallas

Yesterday's game between Dallas and Gainesville drew a good crowd and was well played, but resulted in the defeat of the visitors [15 to 4]. They are not strong enough for the home boys, who are much better players as a whole than the professionals.

Campbell Turner said the next series would probably be with Baltimore, as there was nothing in this part of the country worth playing against his team.

October 7, 1897

THE BICYCLE CRAZE

In the late 1800s, a bicycle craze swept the United States. Riding a bicycle was not for the fainthearted. The most common model was the high-wheel model. The front wheel was the high-wheel, which had pedals for the rider. The front wheel came in various sizes, from thirty-eight to fifty-two inches tall. The back wheel was very small. These bicycles were nicknamed "Bone Shakers."

A pall was cast over this city Tuesday morning about 9 o'clock, when the news was heralded along the streets that H.C. Hyman [of Ashland, Kentucky] had fallen from a bicycle while riding down North Dixon Street and had almost been instantly killed....He died in some five minutes after it happened. [He had borrowed the bicycle from Will Kinne.]

Members of the Gainesville Bicycle Club, 1885. *Left to right*: Jessie Williamson, William B. Kinne, and Jim L. Goben. Kinne loaned to Henry E. Hyman the bicycle Hyman was riding when he had his fatal accident. Kinne was a jewelry store owner and watch repairman in downtown Gainesville. In 1896, he was president of the Gainesville Bicycle Club. *Courtesy of Kinnes Jewelers, 210 E. California, Gainesville.*

While passing along Dixon Street near Mrs. Carmon's millinery store, the front wheel of the traveling machine came in contact with a small stone, which caused the bicycle to turnover, throwing the rider and striking his head violently against the ground.

November 7, 1888

The Second Annual Cooke County Fair featured bicycle races.

The grand cavalcade of bicycle riders, forty-five in number, under the auspices of the Gainesville Cycling club, was a beautiful sight. At the conclusion of the parade Miss Grace Hickson was awarded a gold medal for the most graceful lady rider, and Miss Bertha Patterson was awarded a silver medal as second best.

Then came the bicycle races, and a more successful tournament never took place in Texas. Gainesville riders carried off a majority of the medals, and a Gainesville boy, Edgar Patterson, reduced the best state record for one mile dash from 2:57 to 2:56.

September 10, 1892

Prof. Green Watson's bicycle class is growing. F.A. Tyler Jr. and L.B. Edwards joined yesterday and took their first lesson. Both of them are bright boys and capable of learning quickly. C.R. Smith was in the class yesterday evening and the professor says Smith is perhaps his "perfect" pupil.

April 3, 1897

Organized and "Unorganized" Religion

In 1893, the *Hesperian* provided an assessment of the state of organized religion in Gainesville. The assessment was based solely on the nature of the houses of worship.

The Southern Methodists, the Baptists, the Christians, the Cumberland Presbyterians, and the Episcopalians all have fine brick houses of worship. The Methodist Episcopal, the Southern Presbyterians, the Catholics, the Northern Presbyterians, and the Hebrew all have neat and comfortable frame houses of worship. The negroes also have three frame houses of worship.

July 12, 1893

The *Hesperian* seemed to have an infatuation with the growing Jewish community in the late 1800s. Numerous clothing and department stores and saloons and liquor stores were Jewish-owned. A synagogue was built in Gainesville in 1889, and a Hebrew cemetery was created adjacent to the city cemetery.

The Hebrew fair which has been in full blast for several days under the auspices of the Hebrew Ladies' Aid Society, was equally as interesting last night as usual. A large crowd was present and everyone seemed to take a lively interest in the exercise [a raffle].

There will be several very costly fabrics disposed of again tonight, but the most interesting feature of the entertainment tonight will be the contests for two valuable prizes, one a large Saratoga trunk to be awarded to the most popular married lady, and the other a very costly gold-headed silk umbrella, to be awarded to the most popular young man. The polls for receiving votes for the candidates in this contest were opened yesterday, and a large number of ballots have already been deposited which only costs the small sum of one dime for a single vote.

October 9, 1888

There is a strong probability that the Hebrew congregation of this city will soon build a handsome temple. The congregation comprises some of Gainesville's most prominent citizens and leading business men, and if they make up their minds to erect a synagogue it will be an imposing one. At present they have no place of worship, their temporary temple having been destroyed by the late fire.

December 14, 1888

The dedication services of the new synagogue on Bogg street [now Main Street] commenced at 5:30 o'clock last evening and continued several hours, and were most solemn and impressive throughout. A large number were present, and participated in the forms and ceremonies of the dedication. A goodly number of gentiles were present, and manifested a deep interest in the solemn exercises.

This synagogue is perhaps the finest structure of the kind in northern Texas, especially the interior, which far eclipses any edifice for public worship in Gainesville.

Our Hebrew friends are to be congratulated on their enterprise and success in erecting such a beautiful house for worship in this city.

The dedication ceremonies were conducted by Rabbi Strauss, the home minister.

September 21, 1889

In 1895, the synagogue was moved to the corner of Red River and Broadway Streets.

The rabbis who came to Gainesville were foreign-born and had more formal education than their Christian counterparts.

Rev. A.M. Bloch formerly of Montreal, Canada, arrived in the city Monday and for the next year will have charge of the United Hebrew congregation at this place.

Rabbi Bloch is a finished scholar and a cultured gentleman. He and his good wife come well recommended. Among his recommendations is one from Robert N. May, mayor of Augusta, Georgia, and governor Lowry of Mississippi.

Rabbi Bloch…makes French, German and Latin a specialty. We hope his association with his congregation here may be pleasant and mutually profitable, and we commend him to our people as one who will make a worthy and useful citizen.

September 2, 1891

A novel spectacle was presented at the Denton Street Presbyterian church last night. It was the regular meeting of the Baptist Young People's society, and the pastor [Rev. Harris] had invited Rabbi Marcus of the Hebrew congregation to tell "What the Jews Think of Christians."

Rabbi Marcus thanked the pastor and said it was the first time in this city that the followers of the "Sage of Nazareth" had ever permitted a Jew to enter the holy of hollies [*sic*]. He said many good things and was intently listened to.

Dr. Marcus has only been in America a little over three years and, coming from Russia, the spectacle of a Christian minister inviting a Jew into his pulpit was to him indeed novel.

July 1, 1893

While there was no reported Christian antagonism of the Jewish community, there was one form of antagonism between the Methodists and the Baptists. In 1889, there was an exciting debate at the community of Era between H.G. Rogers, Methodist, and J.F. Elder, Baptist, over disputed articles of faith. A committee of Methodists and Baptists laid down the following ground rules:

Resolved, First, That said disputants shall be required in their speeches to deal with the issue of their stated questions.

Second, To indulge in no personal thrusts or unpleasant epithets.

Third, To make no use of jokes, anecdotes, witticisms, comical actions, and all such conduct as is calculated to rob a Scriptural investigation of Christian dignity and solemnity.

Homes will be assigned to all who desire to attend and a cordial invitation is extended to all.

November 21, 1889

A long-standing tradition, especially within the Methodist Church, was to welcome a new pastor or a newcomer with a pound party, to which guests brought as gifts one pound of a grocery item as a welcoming gesture.

> Last night was a great time among the church people. A lemon sociable at Capt. Bryson's and a pound party at the Denton Street Methodist [later First Methodist] parsonage were the principal features of attraction.
>
> July 12, 1893

And of course, doing their Christian duty, the churches were frequently engaged in moral crusades. One popular target of their wrath was "Silver City," the area of prostitution within Gainesville. Charles Stetson, the "cowboy preacher," wrote a thank-you to the people of Gainesville after leaving and continuing his ministry in Dublin, Texas.

> Be of good courage, my brothers and sisters in Christ. The saloon men and gamblers, prisoners and fallen women are resting upon my heart. Oh, how kind these people have been to me. Oh, how my heart runs after them.
>
>   Wake up, brother preachers, and go help rescue the poor souls of Silver City. Come out like the true man of God and work for the salvation of the fallen souls of your city. Come, do all the good you can and as little harm as possible. God bless the colored people is my prayer.
>
> October 6, 1894

Another social concern of churchgoers was the evil of prizefighting. In the summer of 1895, there was speculation that a boxing match between world champion "Gentleman" Jim Corbett and the British challenger, Bob Fitzsimmons, would occur at the State Fair of Texas. The boxing match between these two did not in fact occur until 1897 in Carson City, Nevada.

A three-day conference of the Epworth League of North Texas Methodist Churches in Gainesville adopted some resolutions condemning the proposed prize fight.

> Whereas, the daily papers predict there is to be a slugging match in this state, and at the time and place of the State Fair and Dallas Exposition, and whereas, this League conference is for lifting up

rather than for dragging down public sentiment, and public and private morals; therefore be it

Resolved, that we protest against that brutal and inhuman sport, and request our preachers and people everywhere to speak and write against the barbarous and disgraceful thing.

Second. That we request our chief executive to use every means to prevent said fight and urge the speedy enactment of such laws as will prevent such fights in our state in the future. A rising vote showed that every leaguer, both male and female was opposed to prize fighting.

June 8, 1895

And finally, the Local Union of Christian Endeavor Societies of Gainesville congratulated County Attorney W.E. Rodgers during his second term for an aggressive effort to remove "the 'curse' [gambling and prostitution] that has disgraced our town for so long."

We pledge our support, both moral and financial to our county attorney, W.E. Rodgers, in his fight to enforce the laws.…We call upon all liberty-loving, law enforcing people to aid him in his undertaking, and we bid him God speed in his efforts.

July 5, 1895

The Christian Endeavor Society was founded in 1881 by Congregationalist minister Francis Edward Clark. It was a young people's interdenominational organization whose members "pledged to lead a Christian life, pray to God and read the Bible every day, and to participate actively in the work of the church."

JOSEPH WELDON BAILEY: "FAVORITE SON"

Joseph Weldon Bailey (1863–1929) was a native of Mississippi. He came to Gainesville in 1888 to practice law. A Jeffersonian, states rights' Democrat, he was elected to his first of five two-year terms in the U.S. House of Representatives in 1890. He gained a national reputation as an outstanding orator, sometimes compared to William Jennings Bryan. Bailey was elected by the Texas legislature to two six-year terms in the U.S. Senate, in 1900 and 1906, prior to the Seventeenth Amendment to the Constitution, which

Joseph Weldon Bailey (1863–1929) was a dominant political figure in Texas between what were known as the Jim Hogg and the Pa Ferguson eras. He served five terms in the U.S. House of Representatives (1891–1901) and two terms in the U.S. Senate (1901–13). He was a States' Rights Democrat and was either loved or hated by his constituents. *Courtesy of Morton Museum of Cooke County.*

provided for the direct election of senators by the people.

Bailey debated his Populist Party opponent, R.V. Bell, at the Cooke County courthouse in 1892, during his first reelection campaign to the House of Representatives. This occurred when the Republican Party in Texas was practically nonexistent and the real contest was between Democrats and Populists.

Wednesday evening one of those little incidents that relieve the strain of political life took place at the store of Schiff and Sommer & Company.

A few of the personal friends of Hon. J.W. Bailey concluded to give a small token of their esteem for him and his estimable wife before they left for Washington.

A few of his friends assembled and Mr. Bailey was brought in without knowing what was wanted of him. E.P. Hill then presented him a solid silver sugar and cream pitcher with inscription.

Mr. Bailey was taken by surprise but he soon rallied and made a beautiful little speech. Among other things he said: "When I return from Washington, I hope to be able to look every brave, true man and pure woman in the face and say, 'I did the best I could.'"

November 26, 1891

Mr. Bell [Populist candidate for Congress] made as strong a plea as was possible for a man to do for such a platform. He was full of fire and earnestness and he made a speech that he need not be ashamed of.

But it is no disparagement of Mr. Bell to say that he was badly overmatched in the debate. It could not be expected that he could cope with the man who during his first session of congress took a front rank among the orators and debaters of the nation.

November 6, 1892

The report in the Dallas News from Van Alstyne that Mr. Bailey had to quit speaking because he was sick need not alarm anyone. He spoke two hours and twenty minutes, which was pretty good for a sick man.

October 7, 1894

PARTY POLITICS

As noted in the segment on Joe Bailey, the real party competition was between the Democrats and the Populists. The Democratic Party was the establishment party in Cooke County as well as Texas and the South. The *Hesperian* had nothing but contempt for the Populist Party.

On the last day of the recent session of the legislature Bob [Robert Valentine] Bell [Populist] was upon the floor making a speech, with the view that the people of Cooke county would hear of it, and which might possibly gain him a few votes for congress, when one of his brother members offered a resolution that Bob Bell be allowed ten minutes after the close of the session to finish his bombastic effort, and that the sum of $5 be appropriated to pay the negro janitor to listen to him.

Merciful heavens: that Cooke County should ever have been subjected to such an insult. If Bob Bell excited such contempt in the minds of a Texas legislature, with what measure of contempt would he be regarded by the United States congress, where statesmen are congregated.

June 20, 1888

If the Democrats of Cooke County will but discharge their duty they will organize into Democratic clubs and stamp out of existence this third party [Populist] movement. They should also refuse to admit anyone into their clubs who will not pledge himself to vote the Democratic ticket. The time has past for admitting traitors into the fold.

June 29, 1888

How to Improve Gainesville

There were a number of things that Gainesville and Cooke County didn't have that the *Hesperian* wished they had.

It has been claimed that a bridge can be built over Red River near the city for $25,000. If this is true the investment should be made at once. The commissioners' court would no doubt aid liberally to the enterprise and our people certainly need it.

June 2, 1891

One of the worst needed things about Gainesville is a hospital where unfortunates can be cared for at the public expense. The poor fellow who had his leg broken last night had no place where he could rest his head, and the poor farm was too far away for him to be taken there last night.

The county physician came promptly, but there was no place to care for him and arrangements had to be made by the officers with no certainty that they would not have to foot the bills themselves. Another of our physicians kindly gave his assistance to the unfortunate when he had no place to go where he could be cared for. Cooke county and Gainesville are rich enough to have a hospital and they ought to do it.

March 5, 1892

We hope soon to have telephone connections with every town in Cooke County. It will be a great convenience as well as of great value.

Take, for instance, the town of Marysville. If a company were formed the total cost of putting up the line would not exceed $35 per mile. The total cost of a line to Marysville would be about $600.

This would enable the merchant or the farmer there to be in close communication with the people here [Gainesville]. He can tell what day to bring the cotton or wheat. In fact he can stand in his store there and make trades to suit his convenience with the man in Gainesville….Should the home doctor have a difficult case and wish to consult a city physician he can call him up at any hour. Should he need the sheriff he can be notified at once.…

What is true of Marysville would also be true of Rosston, Era, Burns, Dexter, Callisburg, Bloomfield, Mountain Springs, Custer City, Coesfield and every other village in the county not on the railroad.

August 1, 1894

The *Hesperian* was concerned about the condition of streets and what to name them. A number of streets today do not have their original names.

"Broadway" is a flattering name to apply to a city street, but then it takes more that the name to justify an appropriation of such a thoroughfare in order to put our "Broadway" in the proper classification of streets of other cities bearing the same title, there should be a few crossings made of gravel at least on that part of the street that passes through the center of the city. The sidewalks connected to it should be covered with a thick gravel coat and the street well graded. It will be in order then to boast of our beautiful Broadway.

January 22, 1888

It was the proper thing for the city council to do when they changed the name of Dye Street to Commerce, and of Hudson to Broadway, and it would be the proper thing to change the name of East California Street to Main. It did well enough when Gainesville was a little trading post on the road to California to designate the way travelers should go by calling the road California Street, but now it is different.

December 7, 1888

Grand Avenue promises to become one among the popular streets and pretty streets in Gainesville. It has recently been graded by the city and now the property owners living on that street are having it graveled.

This spirit of enterprise on the part of the residents will bring this thoroughfare into greater prominence as a result for driving, and besides, this pleasing feature has greatly increased the value of all property bordering on it.

February 28, 1896

The *Hesperian* was embarrassed about the condition of the fence around the courthouse. Gus Meyer was a German immigrant who came to Gainesville around 1880. He developed quite a reputation as a stonemason and laid the foundations of numerous downtown buildings. Meyer also laid some of the downtown's brick streets, some of which remain today.

> That wreck around the court house, miscalled a fence, ought to be carted out of the county. It is a fine recommendation of public enterprise to the prospective business man, who comes to Cooke County with a view of buying a home here.
>
> April 6, 1889

> Gus Meyer has obtained a contract to build a stone fence around the court house. This is an improvement badly needed.
>
> March 6, 1890

Chapter 3

GAINESVILLE'S NOTABLE VISITORS

I t is hard to believe that Gainesville, with a population of approximately seven thousand persons, could attract nationally known leaders, celebrities and entertainers. Two factors encouraged this. Gainesville had first-class opera houses, and Gainesville was easily accessible because of the Santa Fe and Katy railroads.

J. WILLIAM JONES

According to Wikipedia, the Reverend J. William Jones was a Southern Baptist of Atlanta, Georgia. After his time as a chaplain for the Confederate army, he became chaplain at Washington College, later at the same institution which became Washington and Lee University in Lexington, Virginia. He had a personal relationship with Robert E. Lee, and in 1874 he published *Personal Reminiscences, Anecdotes and Letters of General Robert E. Lee* and, in 1906, a Lee biography. Over the years, he supervised the publication of fourteen volumes defending Lee, Jefferson Davis, Stonewall Jackson and the "lost cause."

> Rev. J. William Jones of Atlanta Georgia, who was chaplain of Gen. Robert E. Lee's army, also author of the history of the late civil war and now president of the Southern Historical Society, is registered at the Lindsay House.
>
> January 20, 1888

JAMES BRITTON CRANFILL

According to the *Handbook of Texas Online,* James Britton Cranfill was born in Parker County, Texas, in 1858. He had no formal higher education, but after studying medicine under his father, a doctor, he passed the Texas medical examination and became a doctor in 1879. His journalistic career began with his editorship of the *Turnersville Effort,* a monthly publication fighting mob rule and saloons. Later, his daily *Waco Advance* promoted a prohibition amendment to the Texas Constitution. Later still, he cofounded *the Texas Baptist Standard*.

> Dr. J.B. Cranfill, the "all wool and a yard wide" prohibition editor of the Waco Advance, was in the city yesterday and made the HESPERIAN a pleasant call.
>
> February 25, 1888

"All wool and a yard wide" is an idiom that means "genuine, not fake; honorable."

HENRY ANDREW "HECK" THOMAS

Deputy U.S. Marshal Henry Andrew "Heck" Thomas (1850–1912) was a famous lawman in Indian Territory from 1886 to 1900. He became a legend known for his bravery, integrity and fairness. His most famous outlaw casualty was Bill Doolin. Thomas and two other U.S. deputy marshals, Bill Tilghman and Chris Madsen, were labeled the Three Guardsmen by the outlaws they pursued.

It was because of Heck Thomas's dogged pursuit of the Dalton gang, according to Emmitt Dalton, that the gang left Indian Territory and unsuccessfully attempted two simultaneous bank robberies in Kansas, which decimated the Dalton gang.

> Marshal Heck Thomas, who was in the city yesterday informed a reporter of THE HESPERIAN that he had ten prisoners corralled in camp near Ardmore, whom he will take overland in a few days to Fort Smith for imprisonment and trial.
>
> July 14, 1889

Henry Andrew "Heck" Thomas, U.S. marshal, Indian Territory, later chief of police of Lawton, Oklahoma. *Courtesy of Wikipedia.*

Marshal Heck Thomas arrived in the city Tuesday evening from Henrietta, having in custody a Choctaw Indian named Poley Impson, charged with intent to kill one Mike Flynn, at White Bead, I.T., about two years ago, since which time Poley has been at large, a good portion of which he has spent in New Mexico and Colorado, being on the dodge from Officer Thomas, who held the warrant for his arrest. The Indian on last Monday night entered a store at Henrietta, where Mr. Thomas happened to be at the time, and was arrested before he could make his escape. He will be taken to Fort Smith for trial.

January 8, 1890

RICHARD BENNETT HUBBARD JR.

Richard Bennett Hubbard Jr. was elected lieutenant governor of Texas in 1873 and 1876. He replaced Governor Richard Coke in December 1876 when Coke resigned to become a U.S. senator. Hubbard served as governor until January 21, 1879, during which time the legislature never met. President Grover Cleveland appointed Hubbard minister to Japan in 1885.

Hubbard was invited to Gainesville to promote a proposed railroad between Gainesville and Alexandria, Louisiana. That proposed railroad was never built. Hubbard spoke more about his experiences in Japan than he did the proposed railroad. The other former governor referred to in the following excerpt was James Webb Throckmorton, governor from 1866 until 1867, when he was removed from office under martial law by General Phillip Sheridan.

> Last night an overflowing audience greeted the two ex-governors at the court house. After several pieces of music by the Gate City band, Ex-Governor and Ex-Minister Hubbard was introduced by Mr. R.D. Gribble, who stated that the speaker would speak on Japan and its relations in a commercial point of view with the United States, also in its wonderful development in educational matters, after which he would speak a few words on the subject of the proposed railroad between Alexandria and Gainesville.
>
> July 26, 1889

WILLIAM M. STEWART AND JOHN WESLEY POWELL

The most important group of United States government officials ever to visit Gainesville, headed by U.S. Senator William M. Stewart and John Wesley Powell, explorer of the Grand Canyon and director of the U.S. Geological Survey, arrived in Gainesville on September 12, 1889. They were there on a tour of the West in order to make a report to Congress on the feasibility of irrigating much of the West.

Senator Stewart and John Wesley Powell were already well known nationally. Two others in their group, Charles J. Kappler and Edgar Beecher Bronson will later become well known.

> A special train arriving in Gainesville at 8:30 Wednesday (September 11) over the Missouri, Kansas and Texas from Ft. Worth via Dallas had aboard one of the most distinguished parties that has visited this city in many a day, this party being composed of U.S. Senator William M. Stewart, of Nevada, better known in that state as "Silver Bill" and "Sage Brush Bill," a member of the committee sent out to inquire to the feasibility of reclaiming certain lands lying in various states and territories by irrigation. He was accompanied by J.W. (John Wesley) Powell, director of the U.S. geological survey; Col. R.J. Hinton of the U.S. geological survey; Dr. Hines, the Associated Press; the U.S. deputy surveyor in charge of public lands in Nevada and Arizona; Eugene Davis, sergeant-at-arms; R.S. Boswell, stenographer; Charles J. Kappler, clerk; and P.C. Worman and Edgar B. Bronson.

In their interviews at the Turner Cottage, Senator Stewart stated that West and Northwest Texas should rely on artesian wells due to the insufficiency of rainfall in that area. "The engineers have been instructed to report all public lands needed for storage and susceptible to irrigation to the interior department, and they will be withdrawn and not be subject to homesteading under the present law."

Major Powell was planning to ask Congress for $50,000 to make a survey of West Texas to illustrate the need for irrigation there. He anticipated no trouble getting the money with the support of the Texas delegation in Congress. Powell estimated that half the area of Texas would benefit from irrigation.

> Three big bugs after having stored away something less than a car load of the palatable edibles so well prepared at the Turner mansion, boarded their palatial car and pulled out for Garden City, Kansas, at which place Senator Plumb, of Kansas, and Senator Jones of Arkansas, will join Senator Stewart and they then go to Cheyenne, Wyoming, where the committee will adjourn to meet in Washington about the first of December for the purpose of submitting their report to congress.
>
> September 13, 1889

John Wesley Powell (1834–1902), as a young man, rowed the length of the Mississippi River and the Ohio River. At the age of twenty-five, he was elected to the Illinois Natural History Society.

John Wesley Powell, Grand Canyon explorer and director of the U.S. Geological Survey. *Courtesy of the National Portrait Gallery.*

Powell enlisted in the Union army as a cartographer, topographer and military engineer. He lost an arm at the Battle of Shiloh, but that didn't prevent him from leading an expedition of the Colorado River through Grand Canyon.

William Morris Stewart (1827–1909) moved from Ohio to California in 1850 because of the gold rush. He later became attorney general of California. He moved to Nevada in 1860, where he made a fortune engaged in mining litigation. As a U.S. senator, "Silver Bill" served in the Senate as a Republican from 1864 to 1875. From 1887 to 1905, he served in the Senate as a Silver Republican. He served on Senate committees on railroads, mining and Indian affairs.

Charles J. Kappler (1868–1946) was a staff member of the Senate Committee on Indian Affairs when he visited Gainesville. He later published *Indian Affairs: Laws and Treaties (1904–1941)*, a five-volume work that became the authoritative source on that subject.

Edgar Beecher Bronson (1856–1947) was a nephew of Henry Ward Beecher, abolitionist. Bronson was a New Yorker who went west in 1877 to learn how to be a rancher, like Theodore Roosevelt later. He spent time in Nebraska and later became a west Texas cattleman. His autobiographical *Reminiscences of a Ranchman* tells the story of being the first to herd cattle north of the Platte River into Sioux country.

Lizzie Evans

Lizzie Evans (1864–1923) was a native of Ohio and was a popular entertainer in vaudeville and musical theater, especially in New York and Chicago in the late nineteenth and early twentieth centuries.

> The largest crowd that has assembled in the opera house this season greeted "Our Favorite" Lizzie Evans in her new play "The Buckeye" last night at Hulett's opera hall, and to say that everyone present was

well pleased with the entertainment would only be a very common way to express the universal sentiment of that vast audience.

In fact, everybody was delighted, gratified, edified, and at times were carried away in ecstasies with the happy sayings and cunning conclusions of the little lady. The support of the little star is first class, not a "stick" among them, and it can be said without fear of successful contradiction that this is by far the best troupe that has showed in Gainesville this season.

Lizzie has lots of admirers in Gainesville who are always delighted with her coming and it is to be hoped that the little lady will come to us again in the near future, not later than the next season at the farthest.

February 20, 1890

Ben Stockton Terrell

Ben Stockton Terrell (1842–1928) would later change his mind about what he said in Gainesville in 1890. He was a Texas Confederate veteran from Guadalupe County. Terrell joined the Farmers' Alliance in 1886 and became treasurer of the Texas Alliance Exchange. In 1887, he became a national lecturer for the Farmers' Alliance and organized chapters throughout the South. In 1892, he was a delegate to the Populist Party's first national convention and was an unsuccessful Populist candidate for the U.S. House of Representatives from Texas.

A large number of farmers, members of the Cooke County Farmers Alliance, met in the court house in this city Monday, on business of importance connected with the order, and to listen to an address by Hon. Ben Terrell, of Alabama, lecturer of the National Farmers Alliance and Industrial Union.

Mr. Terrell is a fine speaker, fair, logically and forcibly, and makes no demands for legislation, but what should be granted the farming classes, the most deserving class in the land. The speaker opposed third parties, and said the two great parties at present are sufficient to give the farmers their needed legislation, if the farmers themselves see to it that the right kind of men are nominated and elected to carry out their demands. He had no use for those demagogue tricksters or men who try to ride into public office on the prejudices of the people.

The Farmers Alliance in Cooke County numbers over 2,000 members.

March 11, 1890

JENNIE CALEF

In promoting Jennie Calef and her comedy troupe's appearance at Hulett's Opera House on March 21, 1890, the *Hesperian* quoted the *Richmond Daily News*:

> One of the prettiest sights and brightest little actress on the American stage is Jennie Calef....Her success, phenomenal as it has been, has not swelled her head, and she is today the same sensible, every day American girl as she was when she first appeared behind the footlights.
>
> No breath of scandal has ever been attached to her name and she has well demonstrated that a woman can become a successful actress and still be a lady and true woman.

March 19, 1890

Photographs of Jennie were popularly featured on tobacco company trading cards and on cabinet cards. Cabinet cards were photographs printed on heavy card stock to prevent the pictures from curling up and commonly displayed in cabinets. They were especially popular in the 1880s.

WILLIAM C. GORGAS

Lost

In the city of Gainesville, a small surgical pocket case, surgical case with my name on it. Will pay a reward for its return to me.

W.C. Gorgas, Captain Medical Department, U.S. Army, Fort Reno, Okla. Territory

July 1, 1893

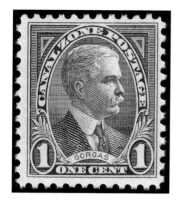

William C. Gorgas, as a young army medical officer, lost his medical kit in Gainesville. *Courtesy of Wikipedia.*

Gorgas later became famous. He was the chief sanitary officer in Havana at the end of the Spanish-American War, dealing with combating yellow fever. His role in eradicating yellow fever in Panama was instrumental in the construction of the Panama Canal. He was later president of the American Medical Association and awarded the first Public Welfare Medal from the Academy of Science. He was knighted by King George of England shortly before his death in 1920.

JAMES HARVEY "CYCLONE" DAVIS

It was probably no coincidence that two prominent Texans both known for their oratory skills, "Cyclone" Davis and Temple Houston, were in Gainesville simultaneously.

James Harvey Davis (1854–1940), an East Texas lawyer, has been described as "a passable writer, but his real talent lay in oratory." He began his public speaking career as a lecturer for the Farmers' Alliance, which was a precursor to the Populist Party movement. He campaigned for Democrat Jim Hogg, a progressive reformer who was elected Texas governor in 1890. Davis was a delegate to the Populist Party's 1892 national convention in Cincinnati, helping write the party's platform. He criticized both the Democratic and Republican parties for being in the Hamiltonian tradition.

Davis had several nicknames. He was called "Cyclone Davis" after he swept away the arguments of an opponent so resoundingly that the opponent refused to debate him anymore in what had been planned as a series of debates. Davis, with his six-foot-three height, flowing beard, booming voice and biblical references, had the countenance of

James Harvey "Cyclone" Davis, a Populist orator who received his nickname for "sweeping away" his opponents. He ran unsuccessfully as a Populist candidate for Congress but was elected as a Democrat in 1914. *Courtesy of Wikipedia.*

a biblical prophet. Thus he became "Methodist Jim," although he was a member of the Disciples of Christ church.

> J.H. Davis (Tornado) will speak Friday, 26th inst. At the courthouse in the afternoon and at night. Mr. Davis is one of the populist leaders and is a very clever gentleman and has considerable reputation as an orator.
>
> January 25, 1894

The *Hesperian* editor interviewed Cyclone Davis and liked him because of the journalistic connection: Davis had owned the *Mount Vernon Franklin Herald* in East Texas. The *Hesperian* editor said he preferred to call Davis "Methodist Jim," adding, "We will always be glad to meet him no matter whether we are together in politics or not." The *Hesperian* didn't cover Davis's speech at the courthouse, probably because it strongly disapproved of his populist message.

Temple Lea Houston

Temple Lea Houston (1860–1905) was the youngest son of Sam and Margaret Lea Houston, but as an adult he wanted to be known for his own accomplishments, not as the son of his famous father. He was a young boy when both his parents died. He became the youngest practicing lawyer in Texas in 1880. Governor Oran M. Roberts appointed him district attorney for twenty-six unorganized counties in the Texas panhandle. Later, he was elected to two terms in the Texas senate, in 1884 and 1886.

While he was practicing law in Canadian, two of his major clients were the Santa Fe Railroad and Henry B. Sanborn (also referred to in this chapter). When in Gainesville in 1894, Temple Houston was a resident of Woodward, Indian Territory, as he had participated in the land run of Oklahoma's Cherokee Strip in 1893. As a flamboyant orator, he probably gave more than one speech at the courthouse here, although that wasn't mentioned in the *Hesperian*.

> The Honorable Temple Houston, Panhandle Senator, is in the city.
>
> February 8, 1890

Temple Houston

Temple Lea Houston, youngest son of Sam Houston, *(third from left)* with a group of hunters. *Courtesy of the Oklahoma Historical Society.*

> Hon. Temple Houston is in the city. Mr. Houston is strong for [George] Clark and has been doing good work on the stump.
>
> May 8, 1892

George Clark of Waco was a railroad attorney and contested Jim Hogg for the Democratic nomination for governor in 1892. He criticized the newly created Texas Railroad Commission, whose members were then appointed by the governor, as being "undemocratic" and created to harass the railroads. He favored the popular election of the commission and allowing the railroad to appeal the commission's rulings to the courts. The *Hesperian* endorsed Clark for governor. Hogg won the Democratic renomination at the state convention and subsequently won reelection.

In 1899, Houston gave a famous defense of prostitution in a court case in Woodward, Indian Territory, defending a "Woodward soiled dove," Minnie Stacey. He blamed men for the evil of prostitution and gained the acquittal of Miss Stacey.

JOHN J. MCCLOSKEY

John J. McCloskey (1862–1940) began playing professional baseball in Kentucky in 1882, usually outfield or first base. In 1887, he organized a barnstorming Joplin, Missouri team that beat the touring New York Giants in two games in Austin. Austin baseball fans encouraged him to create the Texas League, which he did in 1888. He first managed the Austin team and later the Houston team in that league. From 1906 to 1908, he managed the St. Louis Cardinals. He is a member of the Texas Sports Hall of Fame.

> J.J. McClosky, manager of the North Texas Base Ball league, is in the city endeavoring to get Gainesville to join the league. A meeting of the local base ballists were held at the opera house last night, but no definite action was taken.
>
> It is proposed to give Gainesville the Houston team and to open the season with the Sherman club in a series of four games at the fairgrounds on next Friday; the games to be played on Friday [October 7], Saturday, Sunday and Monday next.
>
> October 5, 1892

JAMES W. THROCKMORTON

James W. Throckmorton (1825–1894) was a native of Tennessee but longtime resident of McKinney, Texas. He first had a career as a doctor and later became a lawyer. He supported Sam Houston as an opponent of secession but fought in the Confederacy after secession.

Throckmorton was elected governor of Texas in 1866, resisted Radical Reconstruction policies and was removed from office in 1867 by General Philip Sheridan for violating the Military Reconstruction Act of 1867. He visited Gainesville in 1892, approximately two years before his death. Throckmorton Street in Gainesville is probably named for him.

> Governor Throckmorton left for home yesterday evening after an extended duck hunt here. The governor enjoys hunting as well as he used to when he ranged through this country forty years ago.
>
> December 10, 1892

Henry B. Sanborn

Henry B. Sanborn became a millionaire as a traveling salesman, peddling Joseph Glidden's patented "winner" two-stranded barbed wire in Texas in 1875. Sanborn had conveniently married Glidden's orphaned niece after boarding with the Glidden family in DeKalb, Illinois. Sanborn brought reels of barbed wire from Illinois to Denison, Texas, where the railroad then ended, acquired a buggy, rode to Gainesville and sold ten reels of barbed wire to Cleaves and Fletcher Hardware, the site of the first sale of Glidden "No. 5" barbed wire in Texas.

Sanborn established a model ranch close to Whitesboro nearby to demonstrate the effectiveness of the new barbed wire. Later, with Joseph Glidden, he created the Frying Pan Ranch in West Texas and became the founder of Amarillo.

Henry's older brother, Charles, originally came to Texas to help manage Henry's Whitesboro ranch. He left there to come to Gainesville and open a feed and seed store on the corner of California and Chestnut Streets, where he also sold Glidden barbed wire.

> H.B. Sanborn of Kansas City is visiting C.C. Sanborn, his brother.
> February 3, 1894

Anna Eva Fay

Anna Eva Fay was a nationally known spiritual medium who performed once in Gainesville, but she was a fraud. From the stage, she supposedly could read the audience's minds, but after she retired, she admitted she had planted people in the audience to relay personal information to her about the persons she interviewed.

> Miss Fay does a great many wonderful things, though she does not call them tricks, but rather manifestations of occult power. She comes to Gainesville from Dallas, where she has been a constant subject of talk, the newspapers all making great efforts to discover some hidden means by which she is assisted in her manifestations.
>
> An interesting feature of the entertainment is the talking hand, a wooden representation which taps out responses to questions put to it.
> March 8, 1894

Annie Abbott (Dixie Annie Jarrett Haygood)

Another female performer who overshadowed Miss Fay was Annie Abbott, the stage name of Dixie Annie Jarratt Haygood. Because of her feats of strength, she was nicknamed "the Little Georgia Magnet."

> Annie Abbott's performance last night left the audience amazed. The feats she performed were inexplicable. She excites a wonderful influence over men. To see her standing on one foot, and withstanding the combined strength of four strong men stamped her as no ordinary mortal.
>
> Sheriff Ware thought he could lift her, but concluded he could not. He undertook to put a billiard cue to the floor when she had her hands on it. He broke the cue, but could not put it to the floor. She lifted four heavy men in a chair and held two eggs between her hands and the chair, but did not break the eggs.
>
> March 16, 1894

John H. Reagan

John H. Reagan, nicknamed the Old Commoner, was the former postmaster general of the Confederacy and as a congressman in 1887 was instrumental in passing the Interstate Commerce Act. Progressive governor James Hogg appointed him chair of the newly created Texas Railroad Commission, which regulated railroad freight rates. He was in Gainesville as part of his unsuccessful campaign for the Democratic nomination for governor. Reagan was seventy-six years old at the time.

John H. Reagan, former Confederate postmaster general and chair of the Texas Railroad Commission. *Courtesy of Wikipedia.*

> Saturday was a great day for the Reagan men in Cooke County. The "old commoner" arrived on the 10:30 train in the morning and was greeted by a large number of people at the depot.
>
> Behind him on the wall [in the courthouse] was hung a picture of Jefferson Davis and his cabinet, and Mr. Reagan who looked young and vigorous in that picture, was the last surviving member of it.

He shows weariness, having traveled and spoken every day for several weeks.

Mr. Reagan never was an orator, but he was a logical, accurate and interesting speaker. He is tedious, but methodical, and always makes his points tell. He is a living cyclopedia of political facts…yet never uses notes.

July 15, 1894

Jacob S. Coxey

Jacob S. Coxey was profoundly affected by the Panic of 1893. As owner of a silica quarry in Massillon, Ohio, he was forced to lay off his workers. He decided to march on Washington to protest economic policies that were causing much unemployment. While leading four hundred marchers in Washington, he was arrested for walking on the grass. His march had little effect but gained national attention.

Jacob S. Coxey, leader of the march on Washington to protest the plight of the unemployed during the Panic of 1893. *Courtesy of populistmovement.weebly.com.*

Last night the courthouse was pretty well filled to hear Gen. J.S. Coxey, the populist candidate for governor of Ohio.

General Coxey lives at Massillon, Ohio, and it is said to be well respected by all parties at his home. He was introduced by Hon. R.V. Bell who announced him as one of the most notorious men in the United States. Gen. Coxey was liberally applauded when he rose.

He spoke in an easy fluent manner. He approached his subject cautiously and good naturedly. He was not wild nor spiteful against capital.

He drew a gruesome picture of the foreclosures of mortgages during the panic. He is a rather catchy speaker. He elucidated on his non-interest bond scheme, which he claimed would remedy the evil.…This part of his speech was wild and impracticable and did not take even with all of the populists.

While he is wilder than any man we ever heard on the money question, he is certainly an entertaining talker.

August 16, 1895

John L. "Sin Killer" Griffin

According to the *Handbook of Texas Online,* John L. "Sin Killer" Griffin was a popular Black evangelist of the Baptist faith in the late 1800s. He gained his nickname because of numerous revivals he conducted in North Texas. In 1886, he became the pastor of Antioch Baptist Church in Dallas, and later served as pastor of Hopewell Baptist Church in Denison. His revivals attracted both Blacks and Whites.

> Sin Killer Griffin honored our city with his presence yesterday. He was on his way to Ardmore to exterminate what few germs of sin remain in that metropolis.
>
> December 12, 1894

Albery Allson Whitman

Albery Allson Whitman was born into slavery in 1851 in Kentucky. He published his first poetry collection as a student at Wilberforce University. By the age of twenty-six, he was a financial agent for the university and an active pastor in the South and the Midwest.

Whitman became known as the "Poet Laureate of the Negro Race." Dominant themes of his poetry, which made use of complex rhyme and metrical schemes, were freedom and the representation of a multiethnic American identity.

> Alberry Whitman, the famous evangelist and his company of singers, will open in a big tent opposite the opera house on Dixon Street tonight. Whitman is known all over the country as the poet evangelist of the South. His wife and daughters with other talented singers aid him in his work wherever he goes.
>
> Essie, a daughter not yet 14 years old, enjoys the distinction of being the youngest soloist of her age.
>
> Mr. Whitman comes to Gainesville from Sherman. Speaking of his work there the Daily Monitor says: "Immense crowds thronged to hear him in spite of rain and wind. His audiences were two-thirds white people of the very best citizens of Sherman."

Mr. Whitman cordially invites the white citizens of Gainesville to turn out. Separate seats will be set apart for all who come.

As a matter of course the colored people will be proud to see and hear this noted representative of the race.

June 22, 1895

CARRY NATION

Carrie Nation. *Courtesy of the Library of Congress.*

Carry Amelia Moore Nation (1846–1911) was a crusading prohibitionist motivated by the death of her first husband due to alcoholism. She was born in Kentucky and as a teenager lived in Grayson County, Texas, from 1860 to 1862. After her second marriage to David Nation in Missouri, she moved back to Texas, where she operated a hotel in East Columbia. Carry later moved to Kansas, where she started attacking saloons with her hatchet and became known as the Kansas Cyclone, being arrested approximately thirty times for giving her "hatchetation" treatment.

Carry Nation delivered a very strong temperance lecture at the opera house last night, which was listened to with great interest by the large audience present.

March 7, 1905

Chapter 4

"THE DARK SIDE"

Suicides

The most common method of suicide in the late 1800s was ingesting morphine, or laudanum, which was readily available. Hotels that accommodated travelers were common sites for suicides. The Panic of 1893, a nationwide depression that lasted for four years, may have been a contributing factor is some cases.

Worn Out with Life

If suicide were not so common it would be shocking. That it is so common is more shocking still. Suicide is on the increase, or it at least appears to be, as Gainesville has had a number of them this past year.

The last one reported took place at the Petty building on North Commerce Street. A stranger came there on Wednesday night and put up at the boarding house kept by M.F. Smith. He was a well-built man, about 35 years of age and weighing about 190 pounds.

He had a light mustache and blue eyes and was dressed in jeans pants and a black satin shirt and appeared to be a laborer. He seemed to be drinking and Mr. Smith thinks he did not go to bed at all on Wednesday night. He slept pretty well all day on Thursday and kept up his drinking all night. Friday morning, he did not come to breakfast and about noon one of the boarders noticed him breathing very heavily and called Mr. Smith.

Mr. Smith went for a doctor but before he returned the man was dead. A three ounce laudanum vial was found by his bedside empty. It was evident he had taken the deadly drug with the intent to end his life.

No one here knows anything about him, not even his name. He told the lady of the house that he came from Fort Worth, and left there Sunday. He was taken to the poor farm yesterday and buried.

July 15, 1893

Yesterday morning Miss Rachel Williams, who worked at the Gainesville Hotel, was found dead in her room. She had taken morphine the night before and had died unattended. Her heavy breathing was noticed, but the room was locked and Marshal [Fred] Frazier was called to force the door. She was found dead.

She was almost 20 years old and came from White Bead Hill [I.T.] a few weeks ago. She was a rather good looking, intelligent girl.

What the cause was or why she took this desperate step we do not know. Whether some overwhelming sorrow pierced her soul, or whether life's load generally became too heavy for her and caused her to knock impatiently at the "gates of rest," we may never know.

Esquire Snider held an inquest and will report that she came to her death from an overdose of morphine taken with suicidal intent. She will be buried today in the city cemetery. So far as we have heard none of her relatives have been found or heard from.

November 29, 1894

Rachel is buried in Division 13, Fairview Cemetery.

The gun culture of the time meant guns were frequently at hand, inevitability resulted in many suicides.

Bascomb Brown, living near Sivil's Bend, committed suicide Thursday afternoon. He used a shotgun successfully.

March 28, 1896

The following suicide was rather unique.

A young farmer named Young, who recently came to Cooke county from Tennessee, committed suicide yesterday morning by jumping in a well on the farm of Allen Coursey, northwest of the city.

No cause is known for the rash act. Young was about 25 years old, and has a brother living near the Coursey farm. Justice [Lewis] Rogers held an inquest over the remains and rendered a verdict in accordance with the facts.

April 8, 1897

Saloons and Liquor Stores

A. Morton Smith, longtime editor of the *Gainesville Register*, which supplanted the *Hesperian* as the dominant newspaper in Cooke County, published his popular book in 1955, *The First 100 Years in Cooke County*. In it he accentuated the positive. It is devoid of anything negative, with the exception of the "Great Hanging of 1862."

If all one knew about Gainesville and Cooke County came from reading Smith's history, one would think Gainesville was crime-free, devoid of saloons and prostitutes. Such was not the case. The man who wished to "wet his whistle" had many saloons to pick from in downtown Gainesville.

Excess drinking in those saloons commonly led to fisticuffs. Disputes over gambling debts or over one's beer tab, in turn, led to stabbings or shootings.

There was quite a bloody knock down Monday evening in the beer saloon near the California street bridge over Pecan Creek between Graff, the saloon proprietor, and one Pitner, a stone mason. Pitner got the old larybuck down and gave him a serious choking, and the old Hercules, after arising from his prostrate position, secured two beer-glasses, which he wore out over the cranium of his antagonist, making his head and body resemble a portable slaughter-pen. Both combatants were arrested and put under bond for their appearance in the police court today.

August 14, 1888

The following account is based on two eyewitnesses who testified at the trial of T.M. Upshaw for stabbing saloon owner W.R. "Bob" DeBerry to death. Dick Smith, bartender at Henry DeBerry's saloon (there were two DeBerry saloons), testified the following:

The defendant went from H.D. (Henry) DeBerry's saloon to W.R. (Bob) DeBerry's saloon, on Commerce Street, together with myself, and Upshaw. The first I remember when we reached Bob DeBerry's saloon, Mr. Upshaw asked Bob DeBerry to treat, whereupon Bob replied that he would treat if Upshaw would treat him like he treated Henry DeBerry, that is, pay the account that Bob had against him, as he had paid Henry DeBerry's account.

Mr. Upshaw replied, "That's what I come here for." Bob got a pencil and some paper and figured some, when a dispute arose, and they walked to the front door of the saloon, and on to the sidewalk. A few words then passed between them which I could not understand. Then I heard Upshaw say I am no s.o.b. and about the same time he struck DeBerry with his knife and cut him in the region of the heart.

W.P. Rippetoe's testimony: I was standing in the saloon door near where the stabbing took place....I went to the saloon to pay for a cigar. Bob DeBerry and Upshaw were in the saloon when I went in, and were settling up. Upshaw paid $11.00 on account. DeBerry said there was a balance of $2.40 due; Upshaw said, "I will see about that later," and walked out of the saloon.

Bob gathered his cane and walked after Upshaw. After reaching the door DeBerry said, come back and pay that $2.40, if you do not you are no gentleman. [He was then stabbed.]

December 20, 1889

After a jury deliberated for two days in the murder trial of Upshaw, they voted three for acquittal and nine for conviction. Upshaw was released on bond and very shortly left with his family to go to their home in Oklahoma City.

December 24, 1889

Under the headline, "Saloon Men Alarmed":

The arrest of William Gould, Ed Coopman's bartender by U.S. authority, charged with selling liquor to an Indian, an account of which appeared in Wednesday's *HESPERIAN*, caused a considerable flutter in the city yesterday, especially among the saloon men. Gould is charged with having violated section 2189 of the U.S. statutes which reads as follows:

"No ardent spirits shall be introduced under any pretense into the Indian country. Every person except an Indian, in the Indian country, who sells, exchanges, gives, barters or disposes of any spirituous liquors or wines to any Indian under the charge of any Indian superintendent or agent, or introduces any spirituous liquor or wine into the Indian country shall be punishable by imprisonment for not more than two years and by fine of not more than $300."

The subject of controversy is whether or not a saloon keeper in any state has a right to sell to an Indian....It does seem as if this whole affair is much to do about nothing.

February 20, 1890

The *Hesperian* noted a "first" on March 20, 1890.

A new firm by the name of Kelley and [George H.] Leathers, gentlemen of color, were granted state, county and city licenses Wednesday to operate a saloon in Gainesville. The business will be carried on in the brick building at the corner of Elm and Rusk streets, lately occupied by Mr. John Farthing for a blacksmith shop. This is the first saloon license ever granted to negroes in Gainesville.

Public drunkenness was one of the social evils caused by the saloons.

Yesterday evening a disgusting sight was presented on our most public street. An old man in a beastly state of intoxication was exposing his person in an obscene manner. Women were fleeing from him. We have a law against selling whisky to such men and if citizens can try they can close up the saloon that does it.

January 5, 1894

Saloons and liquor dealers, in seeking advantages over their competitors, advertised regularly. Saloons didn't just sell beer and liquor; they also served food. Ed Coopman, a Commerce Street saloon owner, frequently included witticisms in his advertising in the *Hesperian*.

Free drinks this morning, for everybody at the reopening of the popular Board of Trade saloon on California Street next door to First National bank. Our old friends and patrons are specially invited to call and see us. All drinks free from 8 to 10 a.m.

Joseph H. Embler, Proprietor
January 4, 1890

A cross day with the old lady, or a happy one, the success or failure of marriage for the time being depends on where you drink your beer or liquors—Coopman's has given the most satisfactory results.

July 18, 1893

Although it was a federal offense "to introduce liquor in Indian Territory," the law was not always obeyed. Onlookers at the Santa Fe depot in Ardmore, I.T., liked to joke about all the people getting off the train there from Gainesville. They carried "shoeboxes" of liquor. The bystanders would remark, "There goes some people with 'Gainesville shoes.'" Two Gainesville liquor dealers advertised regularly in the *Daily Ardmoreite.* From the January 12, 1898 edition:

> Max Heyman
> Wines & Liquors
> Post Office Box 317
> Gainesville, Texas
> Prompt Attention Given to Mail Orders

> Kentucky Whiskey Depot
> Wines & Liquors
> For Medicinal Purposes
> Mail Orders Will Receive our Prompt Attention
> [Henry] Waterman & Friedenheit
> Gainesville, Texas

"Silver City" and "Soiled Doves"

Western frontier towns typically provided saloons to quench the thirst of roving cowboys and prostitutes to satisfy their sexual appetites. Gainesville was a jumping-off place for Indian Territory to the north and was situated between the Chisholm Trail to the west and the Shawnee Trail to the east. The expansion of the railroads eliminated the need for long cattle drives, and the coming of the railroads contributed to a more diverse clientele for saloons and prostitutes.

The houses of prostitution were concentrated in an area called Silver City, which the *Hesperian* referred to as a "western suburb" of Gainesville. The

A possible "soiled dove"?
Advertisement for Bertram's
Saloon, owned by Henry
Bertram of Gainesville.
*Courtesy of Morton Museum of
Cooke County.*

area was called Silver City because prostitutes were commonly paid for their services with silver dollars.

A common euphemism for a whorehouse was a *disorderly house* or *house of ill repute*. A common term for a prostitute was *soiled dove*. Other synonyms included *common woman*, *fallen woman*, *cyprian* and *demimonde*. Gainesville prostitutes found guilty of such were convicted of "vagrancy."

> In the mayor's court yesterday, eleven females pled guilty to the charge of vagrancy and were each fined $7.70, or in all $84.70. There are complaints against ten more of the same kind of stock, all whom will be dealt with accordingly.
>
> January 28, 1888

Officer Bozzell arrested "Frank," a hack-driver, last night upon the charge of permitting a man and a fallen female of Gainesville's western suburb Sodom, to ride in a vehicle driven by the said Frank, at one and the same time, and thereby violating a newly made city ordinance, which prescribes a penalty of $25 and the costs for a violation thereof. The party arrested was released on bond in the sum of $100.

The case will be called this morning in the police court, and if the accused is guilty as charged, it is to be hoped that the full penalty of the ordinance will be meted out to the violater. This being the first case to be tried under the new ordinance, it will be looked upon with considerable interest.

April 21, 1888

A young couple arrived in the city from the north Saturday, went to a hotel here and registered as L. Meade and wife of Oklahoma City. They paraded the streets rather conspicuously during the evening, so much so, that the attention of the police were attracted by the wild breaks and cooing exhibitions of the pair, and upon close investigation they recognized the woman to be an old denizen of this city who was in the habit of paying fines in the city court before the halcyon days of Oklahoma.

"Meade and wife" were arrested, she being charged with vagrancy and he with publicly walking on the street with a "common woman." Meade put up $50 in the hands of the city marshal for his and "wife's" appearance in the city court on Monday and then hied away with his Juliet to Silver City to find quarters more congenial than the cops had allowed those to be where the "bridal" pair had first rendezvoused upon arriving in the city.

July 28, 1889

Based on the law of supply and demand—and demand for sex was evidently high—prostitutes weren't required to be beautiful. But according to one old-timer, some of the prostitutes in Gainesville were the best-dressed women in town.

They had a regular jamboree down at Silver City Friday night—a kind of kilkenney affair, and one of the ethereal creatures that tips the beam at 300 solid weight repaired to headquarters and reported guilty of conduct contrary to statutes made and provided, and in violation of the peace and dignity of the city, etc., etc.

The tough old girl paid her fine and entered complaint against two other fallen sisters, who will be interviewed by the cops and escorted to headquarters, where they can be held responsible for the privilege of scratching, biting and pulling hair.

March 2, 1890

One interesting incident that was reported by the *Daily Ardmoreite*, which it picked up from the *Davis Progressive*, involved a town in Indian Territory shipping two "shady ladies" to Gainesville.

A couple of disreputable characters struck our peaceable little city one day last week, having been shipped over the "side door sleeper route" from Ardmore and proceeded to tantalize our citizens day and night. They were persistent cocaine eaters and beggars, and are known as "Cocaine Kate" and "Morphine Jane."

They finally became such nuisances that our citizens took up a collection and sent them south Tuesday evening on the 4:21 train. No doubt at this writing they are in Gainesville having cocaine fits and tantalizing the people of that town. [Ardmore had its share of soiled doves, also; they were concentrated in an area called the Tenderloin District.]

August 7, 1896

The churches of Gainesville denounced Silver City occasionally, as reported by the *Hesperian*, along with the efforts of one woman reformer:

Mrs. Collins ought to have a crowded house at the C.P. (Cumberland Presbyterian) church tonight to hear her explain the workings of the industrial home for fallen women. It is a cause that ought to elicit the sympathy and cooperation of every lover of humanity. Mrs. Collins will do more towards correcting the social evil than all the prisons and courts in Christendom can do.

December 18, 1892

CRIMES OF SEDUCTION, ADULTERY, INCEST AND BIGAMY

The following account illustrates a method of avoiding being convicted of committing the crime of seduction.

Deputy Sheriff [George] Womack arrested John Cody Thursday evening near Ardmore and brought him in yesterday morning and put him in jail. He was charged with seducing Miss Sykes near Callisburg and has been indicted for the crime.

November 24, 1894

There are several ways of getting out of trouble, but J.R. Cody yesterday took the easiest way of getting out of an ugly scrape. He married out.

He was indicted for seducing Miss Sarah Sykes and was in jail awaiting trial. No doubt his conscience smote him and at the same time fear seized upon him. The injured maiden could not be righted by his punishment yet it was but just that he should be made to suffer the consequences of his deed. At last better counsel prevailed all round.

His friends procured a license and he went before Judge [J.P.] Hall with the injured lady and they were made man and wife.

This, of course, did not entirely satisfy the law, but even that stern rules relent in such a case and Cody will go free.

November 27, 1894

Numerous cases of adultery were reported by the *Hesperian*. Perhaps the frontier environment, when a man was absent from his spouse for an extended time, made his heart grow fonder for someone else.

Deputy Marshal Lowe, of Purcell, arrived here Wednesday morning enroute to Paris with a prisoner named Willie Wilson, charged with living in an adulterous state with another man's wife near Purcell. It seems that some time ago Wilson induced a neighbor's wife to come to his lowly cabin where he was butching [*sic*] and keep the furniture in place and prepare his daily meals.

The husband who had been absent for some days during which time the faithless wife went with the handsomer man, returned and went to his rival neighbor and asked for the return of his lawful "rib." The demand so roused Wilson's indignation, that he brought forth his shot gun and made the other fellow cut dirt back from whence he came.

The woman remained with the man who owned the shot gun and there they held the fort til swooped down by Deputy Marshal

Lowe last Monday, who arrested the nester Romeo, took him before Commissioner Hocker, who after hearing the evidence against the man, fixed his bond at $500, in default of which he was remanded to jail.

September 19, 1889

Deputy Marshal Denton passed through the city yesterday morning with A.L. Wilder, who was arrested in Ardmore charged with violating the seventh commandment [adultery], which is also said to be contrary to the statutes of the state of Arkansas.

Wilder was being taken to Paris to be lodged in jail until some of his friends put up the necessary security for his appearance when wanted. The partner in his offense was the wife of Robert Bessent, or it is so charged in the indictment.

Bessent is in jail at Paris charged with some other offense. The meeting between the two will no doubt be an affecting scene.

March 23, 1894

Incest cases were more infrequent than adultery cases. The following case was a complicated one.

George W. Adams, alias Howard, was arrested last night at the Virginia House on Elm Street, near the Santa Fe depot, by officer Morg Faulkner, and placed in jail charged with committing the crime of incest with his niece, Miss Alice England, alias Alice Williams.

Adams and Miss England were arrested by the sheriff last Thursday on the charge of incest, at the residence of J.H. Sullivan, two miles northeast of Gainesville, where they had been in the employ of Mr. Sullivan for some eight weeks. He was doing farm work and the girl doing house work, representing themselves to Mr. Sullivan as father and daughter.

Adams, who was arrested under the name Howard, was placed in jail, and the girl who is in a delicate condition, was taken before the grand jury, but failing to indulge any information of an incriminating character, both her and Adams were discharged from custody....

Yesterday morning a nice looking lady about forty years of age arrived in Gainesville from Purcell, in search of George W. Adams and his niece Miss Alice England.

She represented herself as the wife of Adams, and she has three children by him, and was married to him about 17 years ago, that they formerly lived in Gainesville, from which place they moved to Purcell, where her husband worked at his trade, carpentry, till about a year ago, when he went to California to visit his sister and there he took up with "Alice," the daughter of his sister whom he was visiting, and left California under the pretense of that of bringing the girl home with him to live with his family, but instead of returning home he went to other and various parts of the country, keeping the niece with him....

Mrs. Adams will be taken to the Virginia House this morning by the officers to gaze upon "Alice," and form her acquaintance, after which she will have an interview with the "old man" at the jail, and the probabilities are that peace and harmony will not reign supreme at this meeting. Mrs. Adams says that she intends having a divorce just as quick as it is possible to obtain it.

November 2, 1889

Sometimes a married man might move out of town and remarry without going through a divorce from his first wife.

Charley Scott, a negro formerly of Gainesville, was arrested in Fort Worth last Tuesday and jailed upon a complaint made at Denton, charging him with having committed the crime of bigamy.

It turns out that this "masher" has a wife in this city known as Aggie Davidson, and whom he left some time ago when he went to Denton, where the charms of a dusky damsel of that town captivated the affections of the festive moke and he again took unto himself another rib. Aggie will be one of the prosecuting witnesses.

October 4, 1888

Too Many Wives

Rev. E. Chambers who formerly taught school, held religious revivals and endeavored to peddle out theology in the south part of Cooke County about a year ago was brought to this city Thursday morning from the Chickasaw Nation by G.C. Burns who had arrested him in that country.

Chambers was turned over to Sheriff Ware who placed him in the county jail, subject to the orders of the sheriff of Wise County, where he is wanted to answer the charge of bigamy.

It seems that Chambers took to himself one wife too many some time ago while itinerating biblical lore in that bailiwick and that he was arrested for the crime, and held in bond of $500 for his appearance in district court of that county in due time.

March 29, 1889

Deputy Marshal Jim Chancellor was in the city Saturday morning enroute to Paris, with a prisoner named William Henson, arrested near Lebanon, I.T., charged with bigamy. Some years ago, it is alleged, that Henson married a daughter of a farmer named Jack Spencer, residing some six miles east of Gainesville, where he is living still.

After living with this wife some time he abandoned her, and went to the Chickasaw Nation, where he met up with the daughter of William Moore, formerly of Cooke county, whom he married some two years ago, and with whom he was cohabiting when arrested.

Wife No. 1, her father and the minister who performed the marriage contract between the jilted wife and the "masher" husband, also went to Paris Saturday to testify before the grand jury against the amateur Brigham [Young].

November 10, 1889

SEXISM

The *Hesperian* promoted the stereotype that old maids and widows were desperate in their quest for a husband.

The Somerville Journal intimates that leap year is a sort of wild delusion, because the pretty girl need not propose, and the homely girl is afraid to. Ah, but how about the widow? Fear can't intimidate them.

February 1, 1888

Some of the old maids are getting in their work. One of our bachelors bought a home yesterday.

February 9, 1888

A young lady near Purcell set a bear trap one night last week and caught a young man. What a boon this information will cause to bear traps in Gainesville when the elderly marriageable maids hereabouts learn of the Chickasaw woman's achievement.

December 22, 1888

According to the *Hesperian*, the proper goal of a young woman was to get married and become a housekeeper; therefore, too much education was wasted.

> We emphasize the idea of practical education, for we would not call her educated who returns from college with a smattering of French, music, water-colors, worsted and crochet work—who can parlez vous a little, shine in society, and go through on the piano with some double semiquavers, and yet is ignorant of her mother tongue, ignorant of the music of the sewing machine, ignorant of those graces and accomplishments which qualify her for the real, practical duties of womanhood.
>
> Don't understand us as being opposed to music, painting or acquisition by woman of any or all those accomplishments, as the capstone of a broad, liberal practical training, whose means are ample and talent for their acquirement manifest itself. But we do contend that these should not form the chief part of female education, or indeed be considered an absolute necessary part thereof.

July 13, 1888

Gainesville has a young lady who has not been absent from school or tardy in her attendance for five years. The man who is fortunate to marry that girl may expect to get his meals on time.

June 1, 1897
Originally published in the Denison Sunday Gazetteer, *May 30, 1897*

Chapter 5

COOKE COUNTY

Justice of the Peace Court

What is confusing about local government in Texas is that there are three different kinds of precincts: voting precincts, justice of the peace (JP) precincts and county commissioners precincts. The number of JP precincts in a county is determined by the county commissioners court—not a real court but the governing body of the county. The number of JP precincts varied from county to county, depending on the population density and pattern of the county.

The cases that were heard before the JP court were misdemeanor offenses that occurred within a justice of the peace's precinct. Whereas some cases in city court resulted in incarceration in the city jail, criminal offenses in JP court could result in incarceration in the county jail. Many misdemeanor kinds of criminal cases heard in justice of the peace court were the same as those heard in city court.

> In Justice Snider's court Saturday, John M. Gaugh was acquitted of the charge of illegally using and milking a cow.
>
> December 4, 1888

Unusual cases got the attention of the *Hesperian*: one humorous assault case involved one assailant using a broom as a weapon and his opponent using an empty carpetbag.

In Justice Snider's court yesterday, R.A. Allen was on trial for using indecent and abusive language toward one Edna Kennedy. Some of the evidence was of a racy character and several times the listeners in the court room broke out in a laugh. The jury rendered a verdict of not guilty.

June 27, 1896

One of the civil functions of a justice of the peace was issuing marriage licenses and marrying couples. A *Hesperian* reporter happened to visit Justice Snider's office and found a constable organizing old marriage licenses. Mixed in with the licenses were old love letters written by former Justice H.S. Holman, justice of the peace from 1885 to 1889. The reporter failed to mention whether those letters were sent to his wife, Mary, or someone else.

County Court

Criminal cases in county court commonly dealt with gambling and assault.

The afternoon was devoted principally to hearing of the testimony against some of the boys whom efforts were being made to connect with a scientific amusement, called progressive euchre, and a paste board game called "John from California," but with what success we were unable to learn.

January 10, 1888

F.E. Thyng, the crook who was arrested here last fall, the day the Colvin and Dorris show was here, charged with exhibiting a gaming table, was released from the county jail Wednesday, where he had been incarcerated since his arrest. He was tried and found guilty as charged at the last term of the county court and sentenced to twenty days confinement in the jail, the time having expired. Thyng highly appreciated his liberation, and vowed he would shake the Gainesville mud from his brogans immediately and never more would he return voluntarily to this bumptious burg, whose officers teach the law transgressor the error of his way from a practical standpoint.

February 16, 1888

In the county court Wednesday Annie Scott, a 13-year-old colored girl, was tried on a charge of aggravated assault for hitting Lucien Bone, the young son [he was sixteen at the time] of R.C. Bone, of Bone Brothers, with a brick about a year ago. The jury returned a verdict of guilty, assessing the fine of $5. The costs and fine in the case amount to over $70.

October 11, 1888

Civil cases commonly tried in county court dealt with forced sales to satisfy unpaid debts, lunacy, divorce and practicing a profession without a license.

Deputy Sheriff Bony Apperson sold at constable's sale at the north door of the court house Thursday a piano belonging to Dixie Barlow, alias "Hazel Creeland" to satisfy a debt in favor of C.H. Edwards, of Dallas. The instrument brought $200, and was bought by a Gainesville citizen.

January 13, 1888

E.P. McWilliams was tried yesterday on a charge of lunacy before Judge J.E. Hayworth and a jury composed of W.J. Stone, J.T. Leonard, A.B. Huneycutt, Capt. Anderson, S.J. Kennerly, and A.H. Ross.

The jury found that he was of unsound mind and it was necessary for him to be restrained. He has been acting strangely for some time and a part of his eccentricities have been kept from the public at some time.

But recently he has grown worse and Thursday evening he came to the post office bare headed and otherwise carelessly dressed. He picked up nearly all the children he met and showed many signs of being unbalanced. Sheriff Ware arrested him and placed him in jail as he had been known to threaten the lives of citizens and he thought it dangerous to let him run at large any longer.

He will be sent to the asylum as soon as arrangements can be made to admit him.

August 29, 1891

John Dougherty, aged 74, was tried a short time ago for lunacy upon the accusation of some of his family. But the court found him not guilty. Friday, he came to town and procured license to marry Mrs.

Martha J. Bird, a widow aged 73. He was no doubt in love and the people thought he was crazy.

September 8, 1894

DISTRICT COURT

The state district court is the major trial court, for both civil and criminal cases, in Texas.

The jury in the case of the State v. C.C. Tatum, charged with the murder of Ben Burnham, failed to agree and were discharged yesterday afternoon (Monday). They had been out since Saturday.

What is the peculiar character of the strange delusion that has recently come over certain Cooke County juries? It seems impossible to convict a man any more charged with murder, though the demon's hands are red with the blood of his fellow man, without justification and very little provocation, so far as the public generally has been able to observe.

The man who is tried upon the charge of stealing a $10 pony, by a Cooke County jury is generally found guilty and sent to the pen for five or more years, but the fellow who cowardly takes the life of his fellow man for some slight provocation is seldom convicted. Are we to understand by this that Cooke County juries estimate the life of a good man in Cooke County to be worth less that a ten dollar broncho?

December 18, 1888

Undone & Redone

Mrs. Melinda Mudd, of the Burns City locality, was granted a divorce in the district court Tuesday from her husband, Felix Mudd, and within twenty minutes afterwards she stepped into the county clerk's office where a marriage license was procured and she and J.W. Roark were united in marriage by County Judge Holman.

November 20, 1889

A committee appointed by the district judge selects a grand jury. It is not randomly selected. Below are notes on the grand jury of April term, 1896.

The grand jury was in session twenty-three days and returned seventy true bills [indictments].

A few facts about the jury will be of interest to the members at least, if not to the general reader. Not one of the jurors was born in Texas. Five were born in Tennessee, two in Kentucky, one in Ohio, one in North Carolina, one in Indiana, and one in Pennsylvania.

The oldest member was sixty-four years, the youngest forty-five years. The average age was fifty-four years and ten months.

In religious belief, four were Baptists, four were Methodists, one Christian and one Christian Union, while two were not members of any church.

In politics eight were democrats, two republicans and two populists.

Ten were soldiers in the late war, six serving in the confederacy and four in the union army.

June 9, 1896

GOVERNING COOKE COUNTY

The governing body for county government was the commissioners court, consisting of the county commissioners, who were sometimes called road commissioners, since each was responsible for the maintenance of the county roads and bridges in his respective precinct.

Five convicts were added to the county chain gang Tuesday and put in charge of John Payne, who took them out to work on the approaches of the iron bridge, now being built over Clear Creek on the Gainesville and Denton road. The "gang" numbers seven hale and hearty lads of the genus convict.

January 8, 1890

Letter to the *HESPERIAN*:

The public road interest has almost become a thing of the past, yet we have to use them just the same. I have talked with several of the leading citizens of Gainesville, and all agree that we are all interested alike and should not depend on our puny five day system of working the roads and also say that they are willing to pay liberally to a road fund and put the roads in good order.

This is Cooke County's third county courthouse. The two-story limestone structure was built in 1880 and destroyed by fire in 1909. The first courthouse was a log cabin, which was torn up by a raging bull. The second, a wooden frame structure, was destroyed by fire. *Courtesy of Morton Museum of Cooke County.*

I feel sorry for our county judge for there is hardly a day but what some man is after him about the Gainesville and Decatur Road, and as he is not the whole commissioners court, he cannot control the road funds exclusively and keep up the roads. Now the road from near the south line of Cartwright land to Enderby's is impassable. Now, $500 worth of work and lumber furnished by the county will put this 3 miles of road in good order and we, as farmers, and the business men of Gainesville should rise up and make up the necessary amount and have the roads put in good order at once.

Now, Dallas, Bonham, Sherman, Honey Grove and other places have pride enough to fix up their public roads and why are we so far behind.

J.W. Davis, Era
January 26, 1890

A basic annual function of the commissioners court was preparing a county budget and executing it during the year.

It is ordered by the court that John B. Reagan, Abe Cox, and H.S. Holman be appointed to purchase three spans of mules for the county....

It is ordered by the court that the clerk draw a draft on the county treasurer in favor of Pauley Jail Manufacturing Company for $1,015...for putting in new cells for the county jail.

The iron bridge across Elm and Clear Creek, erected by the George E. King Bridge Company....Clerk ordered to draw a draft in favor of said company for $2,466....

It is ordered by the court that a fence be built around the court house....

$30 each were allowed J.B. Reagan, Abe Cox, D.W. Lewter, and J.B. Jagers, the said commissioner for inspecting and supervising public roads in their respective districts.

February 15, 1890

One Thanksgiving Day turned out to be special for the prisoners in the county jail.

The inmates of the Cooke County jail, through the *HESPERIAN*, desire to return their thanks to the generous and noble-hearted jailer, Mr. Gilley, for the delicious and snowy white angel food and the fragrant and toothsome duck furnished them on Thanksgiving day. Also they desire to thank the YMCA for choice literature furnished them.

On Thanksgiving Day they want to join in with the outside world and thank the Lord they were not in the penitentiary or hanged and were on the praying side of the judgment of the court, and the efforts of the jailer and the YMCA to make the day pass off pleasantly were duly appreciated.

November 27, 1891

Cooke County Poor Farm

There are eight paupers on the county poor farm and five prisoners in the county jail. Pretty good for a county of 30,000 people.

September 5, 1891

Left: Gate to the recently restored county poor farm cemetery on Highway 82, west of I-35. The cemetery's restoration was the Eagle Scout project of Matthew Spaeth. *Photo by author.*

Right: Monument with the names of the county's poor buried in the county poor farm cemetery. The unknown graves were located by James Richards of Richards Monument Company. *Photo by author.*

The poor farm, in the late 1800s and early 1900s, was the county's welfare institution for paupers and the elderly who had no family to take care of them. The able-bodied residents were required to grow crops in common in order to be self-sustaining. Usually, the poor farm had a cemetery for the residents.

> Fred Fountain, a tailor who has been in the employ of Heninger Bros., was sent out to the poor farm last Tuesday by order of the county judge. He was sick and in destitute circumstances at the time, and had no one here to supply his wants. Saturday [August 4] he died and was buried in the potter's field.
>
> August 6, 1888

> J.S. Etheridge was awarded the county [poor] farm for the year 1890, agreeing to pay three dollars per acre for land in cultivation, and the

county agrees to pay him $8.50 per month for boarding and caring for each pauper, with the exception of those under seven years of age, which he is to furnish at $4.25 per month.

November 15, 1889

In company with the county judge and the four commissioners a HESPERIAN reporter went out yesterday and took a survey of the poor farm.

It was a kind of surprise party to the superintendent, who did not know of the visit and was not even there. We found thirteen inmates, all of them more or less helpless.

In the male ward we found Williams, an old Scotchman, nearly blind, who has been there for some time.

John Brawley, a demented fellow who has been there seven or eight years.

Rush Nichols, another idiot, who has been on the county for sixteen years.

Rafe, the old negro idiot, also Willie Quaid, a bright, saucy boy of 12.

In the female ward was Nannie Friend, an aged woman who everybody calls grandma. Millie Hale and child. Mrs. Nannie Mears with three children, and Miss Lillie Barker, a crippled girl.

These unfortunates are cared for at the expense of the county. M. Jackson having the contract for the year which is about to expire.

The male ward is a rather uninviting place, but it would be difficult to be otherwise with the crowd that inhabits it.

We found the female ward neatly kept, the floors and bedding clean. We examined the dining table and while it was not elegant, it was as good as a great many people have at home. We questioned nearly all the inmates, and they invariably told us they had good food and enough of it.

All the inmates seemed bright and happy as it is possible for people to be under the circumstances.

The saddest thing about these unfortunates is the thought that the little girls there will have to grow under such surroundings. Some of the children seem bright and intelligent and under proper surroundings would make useful women. It is to be hoped that the court will be able to find homes for them where they can be educated and trained for usefulness.

It is a work of Christian charity that may well engage the thought of our philanthropists.

August 15, 1893

Pat Ware: "Best Sheriff in Texas"

Henry Patrick "Pat" Ware (1855–1928) had a long career in law enforcement. Prior to his tenure as sheriff of Cooke County, he was first a deputy sheriff and then a city constable. He was sheriff over two extended periods: first from 1887 to 1895 and later from 1903 to 1911. Because of Gainesville's proximity to Indian Territory, he spent a good deal of his time searching there and bringing fugitives from Gainesville back across Red River.

On December 1, 1928—ironically, after visiting the sickbed of Sheriff Jake Wright at the McCain Hotel just east of the Katy railroad tracks on California Street—the retired sheriff's Ford coupe stalled on the tracks. Ware was killed instantly by a Katy passenger train near the passenger depot.

Horse thievery was a common offense for many Sheriff Ware arrested. The *Hesperian* seemed to have great fun in covering the story of "General Mule," accused of attempted horse theft.

> Sheriff Ware arrested and placed in jail a party who gave his name as Franz Hicks. He was trying to sell two ponies on the square which he was offering $12.50 each. This aroused the sheriff's suspicion and the young lad was taken into custody. He claimed to be from Healdton, I.T., but when questioned he could not name anybody of that neighborhood. He also made several contradictory statements which justified his being held.
>
> January 7, 1888

> Sheriff Ware returned from Montague County Tuesday having in charge one "General Mule" whom he had cause to arrest at St. Jo Monday night upon a charge of attempted horse theft in Cooke County. The odd genius who is now in the county jail, has been rendezvousing in and about Bowie, St. Jo, Sunset and other parts of Montague County, where it is said he has not been above suspicion by the denizens of the locality where his mule has been grazing for several months.

149

The general whose last name suggests that his father was an animal of long ears, loud voice and likely mouse color, is a man 21 years old, medium height, long hair, smooth face and minus the left arm. His body bears several scars made by whistling bullets, which he says were poured into his epidermis by Sitting Bull's braves in the Custer massacre, at which time he lost his arm, but if former history be true this mule certainly was not on the Little Big Horn when Sitting Bull butted the yellow haired general, and every accompanying blue-coat into the great beyond, not allowing even a missing mule to escape to bray the alarm.

The general says he is the founder of a secret organization, the business of which is to prevent cruelty to mules. He states that said organization has been in existence for about two years, that it was first organized in Montana, but has since spread over various parts of the country, and at present time its headquarters are in New York.

General Mule was led out of his stall yesterday and taken before Squire Holmes for examination, where his long-eared highness waived an examination, and in default of bond, was remanded back to his stall where keeper Hill will groom and supply him with fodder until the district court convenes next October, when in all probability his royal donkeyship will be sent to Rusk [mental hospital] where an effort will be made to curb his kicking propensities.

June 7, 1888

Sheriff Ware was, himself, the victim of a crime.

Stolen

Some thief stole a bird and cage from Sheriff Ware's front porch last evening about 6 o'clock. It was a brass cage with a yellow singer. The sheriff will pay $5 for the return of the bird and cage or $10 for the thief with evidence to convict.

July 16, 1893

Got His Bird

A great strapping, lazy, buck negro stole Sheriff Ware's bird and sold it to a resident of the city. The sheriff had arrested the negro on another theft and had him in jail when he discovered that the prisoner was the thief who had stolen his bird. He took the negro, whose name is Adams, and made him show where he sold the bird.

These lazy scoundrels who will steal rather than work ought to be sick of it. A few days in jail and a $5 fine have not terror for them. Six months or a year on the public roads would do a thief some good.

July 18, 1893

Occasionally, an arrest by the sheriff didn't hold up.

Jim Anderson who was placed in the county jail some three weeks ago for carrying a pistol had a trial by jury which found the defendant not guilty. The evidence showed that Anderson was passing through Gainesville on his way home in Red River county, and that he had arrived in the city from the nation [Indian Territory], only a short time before his arrest, and was waiting to take the train for the continuation of his journey when, it was discovered by Sheriff Ware that "Jamie" had a gun attached to his hips, whereupon the pistol "toter" was pulled and placed behind bars where he was prevented from creating any consternation among the denizens of the Cross Timbers with his rip-roaring blunderbuss.

January 18, 1888

The Mexican who was arrested by Sheriff Ware a few days ago while masquerading as a woman was released yesterday, no one having appeared to prosecute him, and there being no grounds upon which to hold him. It is said he is wanted in the Creek nation for an offense committed there.

December 9, 1888

On one occasion Sheriff Ware felt insulted by Governor Jim Hogg.

Sheriff Ware was about as mad a man yesterday evening as we have seen. He had cause to be angry, too, and he had plenty of help.

Yesterday morning the sheriff, County Attorney Rodgers [W.E. Rodgers] and Justice Hill wired Governor Hogg that the rapist, Baldwin, had escaped and asked him to offer a reward for his capture.

The governor telegraphed his answer as follows:

"Austin, April 18—Messrs. H.P. Ware et al: Hope sheriff and posse will make arrest in fresh atrocious outrage without incentive of reward. J.S. Hogg."

When taken in connection with the fact that the sheriff's men had wore themselves out in the chase and the man had escaped and the only way to get him was to have officers or detectives trail him up; and when we consider that the sheriff had himself offered a $300 reward for the arrest of Baldwin, we think this telegram was one of the coolest insults that could be offered.

It conveyed the plain intimation that the sheriff knew where the man was and was waiting for a reward to be offered before he would make the arrest. Our sheriff never waits for this, and we do not blame him for being angry.

April 19, 1894

The most spectacular case in Sheriff Ware's career involved the notorious John Quincy Adams "Jack" Crews.

T.B. "Tom" Murrell and wife Anna, and Morgan Murrell their grown son, were all murdered by Jack Crews yesterday morning. Tom Murrell and his wife were shot in their barn near Callisburg. Tom Murrell lived awhile and told the people that Crews had threatened to kill his sons and begged that someone be sent to notify them of the danger.

Morgan Murrell and his brother Len, were working on their father's farm on Red River near Coesfield. Morgan was ploughing, and a bystander said Morgan held up his hands and said, "Don't shoot me Mr. Crews." Crews then shot him.

April 13, 1894

Sheriff Ware immediately organized a large manhunt with four squads of men, totaling forty. It was believed Crews crossed Red River and proceeded west to Montague County where his brother lived. Crews was arrested at a train station near Thackerville, Indian Territory. Crews was tried in Cooke County for his first two murders and found guilty on June 21, 1894.

What our Jailbirds Have to Say

Crews says he was born in Dunkling County, Missouri, forty-two years ago. His father died when he was only three years old. Says he is part Irish, part English, and one-sixteenth Arabian. His grandfather was a half-brother to Jeff Davis' father. Has been married twice. His two wives were sisters. Had one child by his first wife. It is dead. His first wife died in Illinois in 1881. Said he had partially made arrangements with a lawyer named Shropshire in Fort Worth to defend him.

He said he had been misrepresented in the papers about making a crop. He was making a crop at Murrell's. He also worked for wages part of the time. He furnished half the sugar and coffee and they boarded him and his wife and paid him $13 a month for his and her work. Had left Murrell's several times, but it seemed like he had to come back. The only good thing about working for them was that he was sure to get his pay. He "had a good defense," but did not tell what it was.

We suggested that he would find it very hard to make the people believe he had just cause in killing Mrs. Murrell. He replied that Jeff Davis would find it very hard to justify murders charged against him of which he was innocent had he been told just after the war. Said he did not intend to kill Mrs. Murrell, but had to do it.

April 25, 1894

There was considerable stir in the city over the removal of Crews from our jail (after his first trial). Many good people were censuring the sheriff for removing him secretly and in such haste.

The *HESPERIAN* force has been hunting up the matter and trying to get at the bottom facts. The manner in which the removal was brought about indicates that the officers had knowledge of some attempts of mob violence. The sheriff, if he had any such knowledge, keeps it to himself. When asked about it he said he removed him by order of the court....

The judge entered the following order in each of the two cases: It is the order of the court that defendant J.Q.A. Crews, who has been adjudged to be guilty of murder in the first degree, and whose punishment has been assessed by the jury at confinement for life in the penitentiary, be conveyed by the sheriff of Cooke county, Texas, immediately to the county jail of Tarrant county, in the city of Fort Worth, Texas, to be there safely kept by the sheriff of said Tarrant county and by him delivered to the superintendent of the penitentiaries of the state of Texas or other persons legally authorized to receive such convicts, and the said J.Q.A. Crews shall be confined in said penitentiaries during his life, in accordance with the powers of the law governing the penitentiaries of said state.

The first trial of J.Q.A. Crews for murder resulted in Sheriff Ware moving Crews to jail in Fort Worth because of a mob threat to him in Gainesville. Crews's first trial and conviction were ruled improper, and he was found guilty a second time in Denton, where he was sentenced to hang. Shown here is the Denton County courthouse on the day of the hanging. *Courtesy of the Portal to Texas History, https://texashistory.unt.edu.*

Sheriff Ware felt as much outraged at the verdict of the jury [which did not give Crews the death penalty] as anybody, and expressed himself that it was unfortunate for the cause of law and order when they failed to break his neck....

He will be brought back to trial at the next term of the court, and we yet have faith that twelve men can be found with backbone enough to give him the punishment he deserves.

June 23, 1894

A second murder trial in Denton on a change of venue was necessitated because of the disqualification of a juror in the first trial. Crews was found guilty a second time and sentenced to hang. His was the last official hanging in Denton County.

Cooke County News

The *Hesperian* periodically published "good news" from Cooke County towns and communities.

> Burns City, Texas. We have here a very pleasant little hamlet inhabited by good looking and clever people. We have four family grocery stores, two drug stores, four dry goods stores, two doctors, two preachers, two school teachers, and one sanctified man.
>
> January 6, 1888

> Marysville, Texas—March 10—Letter to the *Hesperian*: Our town is enjoying peaceful prosperity now. There is not a vacant dwelling in it, and all our stores are occupied by men who seem to be doing a good business, all except the saloon, and this is closed for want of patronage, we presume. But the saloon's being closed is evidence of prosperity—not of adverse times financially.
>
> March 12, 1890

> Muenster is a proud, growing little place with seven business houses and two hotels. We stopped a few minutes with our friend, Dr. R.W. Crawford. He seems to be the only man authorized by law to roll a pill and his books show $2200 a year and he sells about that many drugs.
>
> January 23, 1895

Chapter 6

NEWS FROM ELSEWHERE

BLOODY INDIAN TERRITORY

A preponderance of the stories coming out of Indian Territory were those of violence. Two murders, separate incidents, occurred at White Bead Hill on the same day. A witness to the first gave his account at the office of the *Hesperian.* A second murder occurred at a poker game a short distance from the first murder.

> E.M. Weaver and John Powers are farmers and cousins. Weaver was assisting at a lemonade stand when Powers brought a friend of his there who had been in a fight to wash the blood off his face. Weaver opposed letting them have water for the purpose, when Powers commenced to curse and abuse him. Weaver walked up to Powers, knocked him down and kicked him. Powers got up and ran to the residence of John Harmon, some three hundred yards from the picnic grounds, where he found the door locked, the family being at the picnic. He kicked in a panel of the front door, procured Mr. Harmon's Winchester, hurriedly returned to the crowd, where Weaver was being surrounded by several men who were entreating him to leave, they believing Powers would return and kill him.
>
> Powers came up, rushed through the group of men, put the muzzle of the Winchester close to the left eye of Weaver and fired a ball into his body, which passed through and lodged against the

skin on the opposite side, killing him instantly. The murderer then walked deliberately back to the house where he had taken possession of the Winchester, took off his hat, fanned himself and viewed the bewildered crowd, which was scattering pell mell everywhere.

He hailed a wagon that was passing near him, got into it, took the Winchester along and compelled the driver to hurry him away; but it is said he soon abandoned the wagon, secured a horse, which he mounted quickly and swiftly left the country.

August 3, 1888

Cal Sugg, benefactor of the orphans' home, was acquitted of murder in Indian Territory on the grounds of justifiable homicide.

A special from Paris of the 19th inst says: A crowded court room waited with baited breath this evening as the jury filed into the court room to render a verdict in the case of the United States against E.C. Sugg, charged with the murder of G.W. Canterbury in the Chickasaw nation on the 7th of October.

When the clerk read: "We, the jury, find the defendant not guilty" the audience expressed their approval so that it was difficult to obtain order for several seconds. The judge then discharged the defendant and the crier announced the federal court adjourned for the day.

Col. Sugg's friends gathered around him to extend congratulations. The evidence was that no one was present when Sugg killed Canterbury. Sugg testified that the deceased married his niece and that she was not living with her husband at the time. Canterbury thought he had something to do with the difference between them and met him in the road, the accused saying: "We'll have it out now," at the same time attempting to draw his pistol, which hung in his pocket. He (Sugg) threw up his gun and fired, then jumped out of his buggy and fired again.

Canterbury fell, but his horse dragged him away a short distance. Other witnesses were introduced showing that the deceased had on two or three occasions threatened Col. Sugg's life.

November 21, 1889

An unusual assault case occurred in Indian Territory, with a Gainesville man the victim.

Yesterday dispatches from Muskogee stated that Frank McDonald, the young dry goods clerk who assaulted Conductor T.H. Conney, of Gainesville, Texas, at Washita station, on the Santa Fe in Indian Territory with a slung shot, made of a weight tied up in a handkerchief, some days ago was tried in the Muskogee court Thursday and fined $50 and costs, and ordered by the judge to do imprisonment in the Muskogee jail one day. The costs amounted to about $325.

September 14, 1889

"ELSEWHERE," TEXAS

Matrimonial news of a Gainesville resident:

Capt. J.L. Cheek of this city left here a few days ago for Indian Gap, Hamilton County, Texas, where he was married shortly after reaching there, to Mrs. Molly O. Lovelace, a wealthy lady of that place. The captain and his bride arrived in this city Tuesday night via the Santa Fe, and will remain a short time, when they will move to Hamilton County and locate on a large ranch belonging to Mrs. Cheek and which goes with the matrimonial prize drawn by the captain in his late transaction with cupid.

January 3, 1889

The *Hesperian* liked to poke fun at Sherman, thirty-five miles to the east.

The old staid town of Sherman is now being treated to a visit of the Salvation Army. It is to be hoped that this sect of professed religionists will continue their journey eastward, as life is altogether too short for Gainesville to think of being afflicted with their presence again.

February 16, 1888

While our citizens are complaining about mudy [sic] streets they should take into consideration the fact that our streets are perfectly lovely compared with the hog-wallow streets of Sherman, where the people haven't sufficient enterprise to put down as much as fourth-class crossings and sidewalks.

February 18, 1888

From the county west of Cooke County:

> In the western part of Montage County, on Wednesday night, H.L. Cherry was sitting reading a newspaper in his house, and all at once fell out of his chair apparently dead. Preparations were made for the funeral and burial Tuesday, but owing to the inclement weather were postponed to next day. Yesterday morning some friends were viewing the remains, and while doing so noticed some peculiar twitchings of the muscles, and upon examination discovered signs of vitality. A physician was called in, and at last accounts the man still showed strong evidence of life.
>
> January 25, 1890

From the town Gainesville envied:

> Paris, Texas. March 30—The first execution under sentence of the federal court since it was established in 1889 took place today when Manning Davis, white, Ed Gonzales, Mexican, and Jim Upkins, colored, were hanged for crimes committed in the territory....
>
> Mrs. Isabella Capps, a white woman of magnificent appearance, who is under indictment for murder and out on bond, accompanied the Mexican to the gallows and held his hand firmly in hers throughout the ordeal.
>
> March 31, 1894

From the *Sherman Democrat*:

> Some of the boomerang throwers with Pawnee Bill's show, which exhibited here last week, got drunk at Greenville and shot up the town with the boomerangs. They were locked up.
>
> September 21, 1895

Chapter 7

TIDBITS

A Woman's Place?

Caught on the Fly

J.N. Robinson, who has been residing in Denton, while near this city Friday afternoon in company with his wife and two children on their way to Indian Territory in a wagon drawn by a span of fine mules, was overtaken and arrested by Deputy Sheriff Spangler, of Denton County.

Robinson was taken back to Denton to answer a charge of swindling a man of $65, and Mrs. Robinson took the lines and whipped out for the Territory in full speed, in order to get out of the state with the team in order to avoid its being attached.

March 17, 1888

A Female Pugilist Takes Charge of the Mayor's Office

Friday morning a woman some thirty-five years of age and tipping the beam at 175 pounds called at the mayor's office and proceeded to read the riot act to Mayor Kirkpatrick in language more forcible than elegant.

What followed was that when Policeman Sid Robertson attempted to remove the woman, he was clawed in the face. She then hit the city attorney in the neck. When the mayor attempted to intervene, he was beaten in the face.

The mayor being thoroughly convinced that the valor's best part was discretion, ordered that the heroine be turned loose by the officer, and allowed to go her way, which she did—when she got ready—and as she slowly retired from the field she shook her clinched fist at the discomforted and bewildered trio and informed them that she would see them another day—which day no doubt the knocked out gladiators hope will never dawn.

The heroine of this revolutionary escapade resides in North Gainesville and the cause of her ire reaching such eminence, was the fining of her husband some fifteen dollars in the mayor's court last Wednesday upon a charge of throwing a dead calf in the street. At last accounts the victor was still at large and the defeated trio was keeping in the back ground out of fear of that "other day."

March 8, 1890

Boys Will Be Boys

Fairly typical juvenile offenses were stealing coal from the railroad and the proverbial raiding the watermelon patch.

It is reported that a number of little waifs are engaged in the unholy business of stealing coal from the [rail] cars, by which business they are realizing a considerable money. Such "kids" should be spanked with a clapboard and sent to the calaboose for repairs.

January 7, 1888

The boys who went to Fount Duston's watermelon patch last Sunday night and tore it up and piled the melons have been discovered, and they live in Gainesville, too. Mr. Duston informed the parents of the lads yesterday of the facts, and asked them to pay the damages for the injury sustained by reason of their wicked boys' acts, and in the event the parents fail to comply with Mr. D's demands, he intends to have the juveniles arrested in a day or so. The urchins whom it is said committed the offense all belong to highly respected families of this city.

July 6, 1888

Of a more serious nature, the drowning of young Tex Potter occupied the news for a couple of weeks; it was even covered by the *Dallas News* and the St. Louis newspapers. At issue was: Did a group of boys murder one of their own, or was it an accidental drowning? There was difficulty in recovering the body, and there were also insinuations that law enforcement officers were negligent in their investigation.

> The boys who went swimming with young Potter were like most other boys, full of mischief, and they engaged in a general ducking. They no doubt ducked young Potter too often and when they found he was drowned they became alarmed. That they did not intend his death is proved by the fact they ran to a school house nearby where there was a singing society and gave the alarm. The natural supposition is that the boys did not know what would be the result of their fun until it was too late.
>
> There does not seem to be the slightest indication of foul work about it. It was an unfortunate and sad affair, but it was nothing more than is likely to happen among a lot of boys at any time. Sheriff Ware is satisfied that there is nothing dark or mysterious about it, and that it was only an accident.
>
> July 19, 1893

Humor

The following scenario could have been part of the script of a movie like *Blazing Saddles*.

> Will Be Captured: The greatest excitement of many years prevailed upon the streets of Gainesville Saturday, when it was announced through a creditable source the Cisco bank robbers were enroute for Gainesville. The officers went to arms and the citizens were busy making preparations for trouble. The bold manner in which the robbers approached the town and the large number of their gang led at once to the belief that they meant trouble of some type and would defy the city officials. It was proposed by some of the older heads not to make their approach known to the women and children as it would cause extreme excitement among them, which would be

a hindrance to cool and deliberate action upon the part of the men. As the rumor had become to be a fact and the bandits were near the city limits, a posse was sent to stop their approach and arrest them, if possible. The posse having approached near and interrupted them, they at once informed the officers that they meant no harm to the city and its inhabitants but only wished to avail themselves of the cheap goods being sold at the Tennessee store.

February 26, 1888

Mixed up days of the week:

A farmer residing in the Spring Creek community came to Gainesville last Sunday with two loads of wheat, thinking the time a week day, and he did not learn of his mistake till after he had driven his wagons up to Brady's mill, and had made the inquiry as to the whereabouts of the millers, saying he thought it darned strange that business men should close up their place of business on a business day.

He was told that the business always closed down on the Sabbath. "Sabbath," he shouted, "this is not Sunday is it? Why I thought it was Wednesday." Upon being convinced that it was the Lord's Day, he drove his wagons into a wagon yard, placed the grain of two loads on one wagon, which he left in the care of his hired man, and he took the empty vehicle and struck a bee line for home to inform his wife of the capital joke he had perpetrated upon himself.

But imagine his surprise when he reached home and found the week's washing on the clothes-line, which his wife had put out that day, she having mistaken the time of her regular weekly wash day. Jim's neighbor says it will be many a day before they quit "guying" him about putting in seven days a week at hard labor. They recommend as a remedy for the "break," a close study of Ayer's 1890 almanac.

February 20, 1890

Another example of the *Hesperian*'s disparagement of women:

The only fellow we have heard who says advertising don't pay is the one who advertised for a wife and got her.

January 7, 1892

ADVERTISEMENTS

This was the era of peddling and advertising of patent medicines that claimed to cure all kinds of maladies, commonly featuring testimonials from those who had been "cured."

> Benjamin Morris, Atlanta, Georgia—I suffered years from syphilitic blood poison which refused to be cured by all treatment. Physicians pronounced it a hopeless case. I had no appetite. I had pains in hips and joints and my kidneys were diseased. My throat was ulcerated and my breast a mass of running sores. In this condition I commenced a use of B.B.B. (Botanic Blood Balm). It healed every ulcer and sore and cured me completely within two months.
>
> January 1, 1889

A much-repeated advertisement:

> A lady was so reduced in flesh last summer by the chills that she actually had to wear suspenders to hold her corset up. Some friend advised her to take Cheatham's Tasteless Chill Tonic—she did so. That pair of suspenders for sale cheap. She now tips the beam at 140 lbs.
>
> August 25, 1891

> General Grant's Death
>
> Was due to smoking a cigar made by a man who had throat disease—so the doctors say.
>
> DO YOU KNOW that many cigar makers moisten cigar tips with their saliva?
>
> DO YOU KNOW that you run a big chance in smoking strange cigars?
>
> Two points are embodied in SMOKETTES CIGARS: PURITY—QUALITY
>
> Absolutely the best 5 cent smoke on earth. Try one. Sold by all dealers.
>
> June 18, 1893

Mayor J.R. Shortridge gave his endorsement of the following cure. He died almost two and a half years later at the age of fifty-three. J.G. Moss, Confederate veteran, died approximately three months after this advertisement.

READ THIS

Gainesville, Tex., April 15, 1897—We, the undersigned, have used Hall's Discovery for kidney and bladder troubles, and have been cured or greatly benefitted by its use and can fully recommend it to others.

J.R. Shortridge, Mayor

R.C. Cook, Ex-County Commissioner [Cooke County]

J.G. Moss

May 26, 1897

BIBLIOGRAPHY

Acheson, Sam Hanna. *Joe Bailey, the Last Democrat.* New York: Macmillan, 1932.

Flusche, A. "Tony" C. *Sketch of the German Catholic Colonies in North Texas.* An unpublished manuscript in the Cooke County Library, Gainesville, Texas.

Fugate, Francis L., and Roberta B. *Roadside History of Oklahoma.* Missoula, MT: Mountain Press Publishing Company, 1991.

Gainesville Daily Hesperian. 1888–97.

Handbook of Texas Online. https://www.tshaonline.org/handbook.

Johnson, Neil R. *The Chickasaw Rancher.* Boulder: University Press of Colorado, 2001.

Melugin, Ron. *Heroes, Scoundrels and Angels: Fairview Cemetery of Gainesville, Texas.* Charleston, SC: The History Press, 2010.

Neeley, Bill. *The Last Comanche Chief: the Life and Times of Quanah Parker.* New York: John Wiley & Sons, 1995.

O'Brien, Robert. *The Encyclopedia of the South.* New York: Smithmark, 1992.

Oklahoma Historical Society. The Encyclopedia of Oklahoma History and Culture. https://www.okhistory.org/publications/encyclopediaonline.

Smith, A. Morton. *The First 100 Years in Cooke County.* San Antonio: Naylor Company, 1955; 2nd printing, 1976.

Texas Almanac. "City Population History from 1850 to 2000." CityPopHist web.pdf

Texas Almanac 2020–2021. Austin: Texas State Historical Association, 2020.

University of North Texas Libraries. Portal to Texas History. https://texashistory.unt.edu.

University of North Texas Libraries and Oklahoma Historical Society. Gateway to Oklahoma History. https://gateway.okhistory.org.

INDEX

McCallum, J.G. 88
McCallum, May 87, 88
McCaully, C.T. 25
McCloskey, John J. 120
McDonald, Frank 158
McFarren, J.R. 77
McKinney, J.W. 90
McMahan, Will 65
McWilliams, E.P. 142
Meade, L. 133
Means, Mrs. Joe 96
Mears, Nannie 148
Medley, A. 26
Meyer, Gus 108
Moffett, Ned 95
Moody, M.A. 27
Moore, Ben S. 59
Moore, Charlie E. 59, 60
Moore, Mrs. Jane P. 66
Moore, William 138
Morris, Benjamin 164
Moss, H. 26
Moss, J.G. 164, 165
Mudd, Felix 143
Mudd, Melinda 143
Murray, Frank 25
Murrell, Anna 152, 153
Murrell, Len 152
Murrell, Morgan 152
Murrell, T.B. "Tom" 152

N

Newsome, Billy 89
Nichols, Rush 148

O

Odell, Minnie 27

P

Paddock, C.H. 36, 47, 85, 86
Paddock, Charles William 86, 88
Parker, Quanah 71
Parsons, J.M. 40
Patrick, Hazel 56
Patterson, Bertha 98
Patterson, Edgar 98
Payne, John 144
Peery, Nellie 85
Peery, Tom 20
Pendleton, George C. 93
Petty, W.P. 82
Phillips, J.W. 89
Pirtle, J.T. 31
Plemons, Miss A.M. 28
Plemons, R.H. 28
Potter, C.C. 89
Potter, C.L. 36, 92, 93
Potter, Dixie Crooks 92
Potter, Tex 162
Pounds, J. Leon 32
Powell, John Wesley 112, 113
Powers, John 156
Praigg, Myrtle 67
Praigg, T.M. 67
Price, Lewis 49
Pringle, J.M. 77
Pryor, Kate 81
Puckard, Ira B. 47
Pugh, N.P. 66

ABOUT THE AUTHOR

Photo by David Moore.

R on Melugin is professor emeritus at North Central Texas College in Gainesville, where he taught from 1965 through 2016. He holds a master of arts degree in history with a minor in government from Texas A&M University–Commerce. He is a member and former chairman of the Cooke County Historical Commission, a division of the Texas Historical Commission. His research has resulted in sixteen Official Texas Historical Markers. His previously published book is *Heroes, Scoundrels and Angels: Fairview Cemetery of Gainesville, Texas* (The History Press, 2010).